Martin L. Brenner
The Song of the Sea: Ex 15:1—21

Beihefte zur Zeitschrift für die alttestamentliche Wissenschaft

Herausgegeben von
Otto Kaiser

Band 195

Walter de Gruyter · Berlin · New York
1991

Martin L. Brenner

The Song of the Sea:
Ex 15:1—21

Walter de Gruyter · Berlin · New York
1991

BS
1110
237
v.195

G

♾ Printed on acid-free paper which falls
within the guidelines of the ANSI to ensure
permanence and durability.

Library of Congress Cataloging-in-Publication Data

Brenner, Martin L.
  The song of the sea : Ex. 15:1-21 / Martin L. Brenner.
       p.   cm. — (Beihefte zur Zeitschrift für die alttesta-
mentliche Wissenschaft, ISSN 0934-2575 ; Bd. 195)
    Revision of thesis (doctoral) — Angelicum, Rome, 1988.
    Includes bibliographical references.
    ISBN 3-11-012340-1 (Berlin) — ISBN 0-89925-721-6 (N.Y.)
    1. Bible. O.T. Exodus XV. 1-21 — Criticism, interpretation,
etc. 2. Bible. O.T. Exodus XV. 1-21 — Authorship. I. Title.
II. Series: Beihefte zur Zeitschrift für die alttestamentliche
Wissenschaft ; 195.
BS410.Z5   vol. 195
[BS1245.2]
222'.1206 — dc20
                                                    91-145
                                                    CIP

Deutsche Bibliothek Cataloging in Publication Data

Brenner, Martin L.:
The song of the sea : Ex 15:1-21 / Martin L. Brenner. — Berlin ;
New York : de Gruyter, 1991
    (Beihefte zur Zeitschrift für die alttestamentliche Wissenschaft ;
    Bd. 195)
    Zugl.: Rom, Angelicum, Diss., 1988
    ISBN 3-11-012340-1
NE: Zeitschrift für die alttestamentliche Wissenschaft / Beihefte

ISSN: 0934-2575
© Copyright 1991 by Walter de Gruyter & Co., D-1000 Berlin 30.

All rights reserved, including those of translation into foreign languages. No part of this
book may be reproduced or transmitted in any form or by any means, electronic or
mechanical, including photocopy, recording, or any information storage and retrieval system,
without permission in writing from the publisher.
Printed in Germany
Printing: Werner Hildebrand, Berlin 65
Binding: Lüderitz & Bauer, Berlin 61

91-B17818

PREFACE

This work began as a seminar presentation at the Angelicum in 1983. Since then it became a licence thesis, a doctoral dissertation, and now a monograph. After so much time I am a little hesitant to let it go out to meet the cold hard world on its own, but you cannot hold on forever. So I present it for the inspection of all and stand back to watch.

I would like to take the opportunity to thank those who helped it along. Fr. Sansoni gave encouragement and support at the seminar and licence level. Fr. P. Zerafa did likewise when it grew to a doctoral thesis. He and Fr. J. Agius levelled objections against it and suggestions for it that have improved it, without doubt.

I give an affectionate thank you to Sr. Mary Ellen Doyle, Sr. Mary Ransom, and Sr. Claudette Hudalla for their efforts in proof reading it when it was still in the doctoral stage and the encouragement they gave to me seek publication. With a grateful heart I acknowledge the generosity of my translators, who helped me through innumerable German articles, Reto Nye, Fr. Frank Sirovic, and Willie Eck.

All one can ever want is that what he has done be of the truth and of some help to others. It is in that spirit that I offer this work on the Song of the Sea.

Rome, November 25, 1990   Martin Brenner

TABLE OF CONTENTS

INTRODUCTION

The Song of the Sea, Ex 15:1-21, has been a question mark in biblical research throughout much of the twentieth century. It has fallen under the scrutiny of many of the most famous biblicists, but still there exists a very great diversity of opinions concerning very basic questions. Estimates as to the age of composition among recent authors extend from the amphictyonic period to the post-exile. There is no opinion which has won consent concerning its place in the tradition development of the Reed Sea event nor how it relates to any of the four major Pentateuchal sources. The question of authorship has been barely touched upon. Most agree that it is cultic in nature, but there is still diversity of opinion regarding its form and the feast for which it may have been written. The search for historical indicators within the psalm has led to conclusions that vary from the thirteenth century to the post-exile. The solution to the historical critical problem, in the sense of what events the Song spoke to and explained for its contemporaries when it was written, starts with the opinion that the Song was of Mosaic authorship and sung on the actual occasion of the victory--it explained what had just happened. And the opinions stretch to the notion that the building talked about in v 18 is the second temple.

The problems involved with the Song of the Sea have a far wider import than the simple placement of this one piece comprising a psalm of eighteen verses and a prose outline involving three more. It touches on the whole question of the development of the Reed Sea tradition. The entrance of the myth systems of

the ancient Near East into Israel's literature and the mode of
their use is of particular import in the investigation. There are
also key methodological considerations inherent in the treatment
of this piece. How is the interior comparison to other Biblical
material and exterior comparison to extra-biblical poetry to be
coordinated so that coherent conclusions can be reached that
pay sufficient attention to the whole gamut of data?

The present work seeks to address most of the extant problems
concerning the Song of the Sea. The questions of the time and
place of composition, authorship, cult nature, theology, and
sources will all be spoken to. I shall seek to take account of the
acquisitions of the previous research. My method pays strict
attention to stylistic devices and forms. Tradition tracing is also
heavily used. Ultimately, the historical indicators have the final
authority in all of the conclusions reached.

CHAPTER ONE
THE ARGUMENT AND ITS DEVELOPMENT

The State of the Research

In this present resume of the state of the question, I wish to outline the major types of methods used to attack the problem. No one author confines himself to any one of these methodologies; rather they seek by a combination of them to place the Song. But by treating the methods distinctly I have sought to bring out what the major questions are, what difficulties are involved in the solutions heretofore offered, and what are the acquisitions of modern research that will have to enter into any answer to the problems.

The treatments of the dating of the Song of the Sea fall into the following categories:

Lexicographical studies

A. Bender[1] and F. Foresti[2] have done studies that cover the entire vocabulary of the Song. Bender concludes from the large number of exclusively late usages and from a series of Aramaisms that he finds there that the work is post-exilic. Foresti also finds that an appreciable number of words in the vocabulary appear only in the exile and post-exile. He discounts the Aramaisms found by Bender, as do all of the modern writers,

1 Adolf Bender, "Das Lied Exodus 15," *Zeitschrift für die alttestamentliche Wissenschaft* 23 (1903): 1-48.
2 Fabrizio Foresti, "Composizione e Redazione Deuteronomistica in Ex 15,1-18," *Lateranum* 48 (1982): 41-69.

but he in his turn finds a rather extensive number of his own. He concludes that the general tenor of the vocabulary is rather post-exilic but will opt for the exile because of a special relationship that he perceives between the vocabulary of the Song and that of the Deuteronomistic redactor of Jeremiah.

R. Tournay and T. C. Butler have both included partial lexicographical studies in their works. Tournay concludes that the vocabulary is late. He opts for the late pre-exile because of words found in the Song that appear only in literature of the period of Josiah[3]. Butler also finds that the vocabulary is late and the late pre-exile to be the most likely time of composition[4].

There are a large number of variables that enter into this method. It is not always easy to arrive at agreement concerning the dating of the other texts in which a specific word appears. That problem is particularly acute when this method is applied to the Song of the Sea. Much of the vocabulary is found in psalmic compositions about which there is little critical agreement. Bender's work reflects a very strong prejudice for the late dating of psalms, and to be psalmic, in his mind, is to be late. Foresti tries to use the best modern opinions on psalm dating, but the problem remains.

And even when it can be shown with reasonable certainty that all the other occurrences of the single word are late, it does not necessarily have to have the weight of evidence. If a word appears elsewhere only a limited number of times, then it may be just accidental that it is not found in an early period. The difficulty is apparent in Tournay's work. He tries to establish that the vocabulary is one which occurs only in the Josian

---

3   R. Tournay, "Recherches sur la Chronologie des Psaumes," *Revue Biblique* 65 (1958): 321-357.

4   Trent Craver Butler, "'The Song of the Sea': Exodus 15:1-18: A Study in the Exegesis of Hebrew Poetry," diss., Vanderbilt U, 1972, 239-247.

period, but he limits himself to just a part of the vocabulary, and then the words treated may have only a few occurrences.

The value of this type of study increases when one word has a considerable number of occurrences that fall into a pattern of late usage. It also is more probative when a large number of the words within the vocabulary of a piece demonstrate this phenomenon of only late appearance. Foresti, for example, has found that a considerable number of words in the vocabulary show elsewhere only in late pieces. And some of these words meet the requirement of having a large number of appearances.

Evidence can also be garnered from theological usages of words, applications of words that fall into a pattern in a certain period. Again, Foresti has claimed to uncover a considerable number of these usages that fall exclusively into late literature. The evidence from purely lexicographical studies does have some probative value in the dating discussion. All who have done this type of work have recognized the late character of the vocabulary. Still, the information to be gained is limited and is usually joined to some other type of dating consideration.

Comparative studies

Investigations of how the Song relates to other compositions in the Old Testament have entered into the discussions of virtually all who have written on this subject. The comparison is usually between phrases occurring in the Song and in some other Old Testament piece or pieces. For example, both P. Haupt and C. Cornill have seen that Neh 9 has some of the same phrasing as the Song[5]. M. Rozelaar, Foresti, and D. N. Freedman will all

---

5   Paul Haupt, "Moses' Song of Triumph," *American Journal of Semitic Languages* 20 (1904): 149-172; Carl Cornill, *Introduction to the Canonical Books of the Old Testament,* trans. G. H. Box (New York: Putnam's, 1907) 540.

note the strong similarity of phrasing that is shared by the Song and Ps 78[6].

Although there are cases where the phrasing is so close that a relationship of dependency can be shown to exist, there are a host of problems attached to arriving at a date of composition. The work itself may have a very wide spectrum of opinions associated with it. For example, Ps 78 is notoriously resistant to critical agreement concerning its dating. Freedman holds Ps 78 to be from the tenth or ninth century, and will maintain that it postdates the Song of the Sea, thus confirming his theory of very early dating[7]. Rozelaar will hold that the psalm comes from the end of the monarchy and will consider it the *terminus ad quem* for the Song, which he dates from the monarchic period. Foresti will place the psalm in the exile and considers that it depends on the Song, which is also exilic. In all the cases, Ps 78 is held to depend on the Song, but a common defect in all these works is that no criterion is given to establish the direction of the line of dependency between the Song and Ps 78.

In regard to the dating of Neh 9 there is no disagreement as to it post-exilic composition, but the problem of the direction of dependency remains. Haupt holds that Neh 9:11 did not know the Song, and thus acts as the *terminus a quo*. He then dates the Song to around 350. But Cornill takes the Neh text as the *terminus ad quem*. Both will maintain that the Song and Neh 9 are contemporaneous in terms of a general period, but this does not necessarily follow. Proponents of early dating could

---

6   Marc Rozelaar, "The Song of the Sea," *Vetus Testamentum* 2 (1952): 221-228; David Noel Freedman, "Early Israelite History in the Light of Early Israelite Poetry," *Pottery, Poetry, and Prophecy: Studies in Early Hebrew Poetry* (Winona Lake, Indiana: Eisenbrauns, 1980) 140.

7   David Noel Freedman, "Divine Names and Titles in Early Hebrew Poetry," *Pottery, Poetry, and Prophecy: Studies in Early Hebrew Poetry* (Winona Lake, Indiana: Eisenbrauns, 1980) 118.

argue that the period after the return was one of revival of ancient traditions and that Neh 9 is making a literary quotation from a very ancient piece.

Another deficiency in the studies that have been carried out to this point is that they have based their conclusions on the Song's relation to only a small number of the works that have phrasing in common with it. No one as yet has looked at all the indisputable instances of common phrasing and tried to form a theory of dating that takes the whole of them into account.

Others have seen a relationship between the Song and various genres of literature. Rozelaar notes a connection between the Song and the confessional literature of Israel as exemplified by Dt 26:5b-9 which he then takes as the *terminus a quo*. Also H. Strauss includes the Song in the general character of confessional literature, but he considers that the Song had a very long history of development that extended into the post-exile[8].

If it is granted that a relationship between the Song and confessional literature exists, it still does not resolve the problem of the ultimate placement of the Song. The relationship to Dt 26 is one of a very general similarity of form: deliverance from Egypt and entrance into Canaan, and this form was in use in the Israelite cult until New Testament times.

J. Schreiner places the Song within the general tradition stream of Exodus-Entrance, and includes the Song within the genre of historical psalms which have this as their central theme, Ps 78, 105, 106, 135, 136. The Song holds best to the theme and lacks the didactic quality of Ps 78; therefore it is the oldest of them. He places it at the end of the monarchy[9].

---

8   Hans Strauss, "Das Meerlied des Mose--ein 'Siegeslied' Israels?" *Zeitschrift für die alttestamentliche Wissenschaft* 97 (1985): 103-109.

9   Josef Schreiner, *Sion-Jerusalem Jahwe's Königssits.* Studien sum Alten und Neuen Testament 7 (Munich: Kosel-Verlag, 1963).
    The positions of German authors whose works have not been translated

Again, it can be granted a special relationship between the Song and these psalms exists, but it does not follow that the Song itself is of the historical resume genre. Also, there is no hard evidence offered to place the Song as the oldest of this group.

Comparisons can also be made between the Song and the kingship of Yahweh genre. J. Rylaarsdam maintains that the real concern is Yahweh's rule in Jerusalem[10]. S. Mowinckel fits the Song into the enthronement psalm mold[11]. Both will then place the Song sometime in the monarchy. G. Fohrer denies that the Song pertains to an enthronement festival, but he does place it within the tradition of Yahweh ruling from Jerusalem, and therefore under the general influence of Deutero-Isaiah. Thus he will arrive at a post-exilic dating[12]. Rylaarsdam holds that Yahweh's rule from Jerusalem is the Song's central theme, and concludes to a dating somewhere during the monarchy, noting that the Deuteronomic period is commonly proposed. F. M. Cross points up the existence of the notion in early texts that God is king and compares the Song with myth texts from Ugaritic literature that proclaim that Baal is king. Thus, the notion that Yahweh is king will play a part in the very early placement of the Song[13].

---

into English are given in this chapter as presented in the admirable summary found in Butler, Song 1-47. Exceptions are the works of A. Bender and H. Strauss. These and the German works in the rest of the book I have examined with the help of translators.

10 J. Coert Rylaarsdam, "The Book of Exodus," *The Interpreter's Bible*, vol. 1 (Nashville: Abingdon, 1952) 940-6.

11 Butler, Song 14.

12 Georg Fohrer, *Uberlieferung und Geschichte des Exodus*, Beihefte, Zeitschrift für die alttestamentliche Wissenschaft 91 (Berlin: Alfred Topelmann, 1964) 110ff.

13 Frank Moore Cross, "The Divine Warrior in Israel's Early Cult," *Biblical Motifs*, ed. A. Altmann, Lown Institute Studies and Texts 3 (Cambridge, Mass.: Harvard, 1966): 40f; "The Song of the Sea and Canaanite Myth," *Canaanite Myth and Hebrew Epic: Essays in the History of the Religion of Israel* (Harvard, 1973) 142.

Comparisons to extra-biblical poetry

In an attempt to escape the uncertainty which has resulted from interior biblical comparison, Cross and Freedman, following the lead of W. F. Albright, have compared Hebrew poetry to Ugaritic poetry. They hope to arrive at a method for dating early Hebrew poetry in general[14]. Inasmuch as a piece of Hebrew poetry conforms to the canons of Ugaritic prosody, it can be termed ancient. The Song is just one instance, albeit a very important one, of the general use of this system. The Song of the Sea more than any other piece of Israelite poetry conforms to the canons of Ugaritic prosody. Indicators would be the mixed meter, complex strophic structure, and the intense parallelism found throughout. Also of importance is an observation taken over from J. Muilenburg that the form of the refrains found in vv 5, 11, 16b, duplicates the refrain form found in Ugaritic myth poetry[15].

Allied to this attempt to use Ugaritic prosody to achieve objective dating for the Song of the Sea, is their study of the frequency of occurrence of archaic orthography. The Song is more consistently archaic than any other work in the scriptures. The orthography indicates that the tenth century is the *terminus ad quem* for the written form, but the original poem is much earlier.

Cross then postulates a common cultural ambit that included both Ugarit and Israel. He also theorizes a very early period of the use of Ugaritic myth in Israel. Then he makes key connections

---

14 Frank Moore Cross and David Noel Freedman, "The Song of Miriam," *Journal of Near Eastern Studies* 14 (1955): 237-250; Freedman, "Divine Names" 77-79.
15 David Noel Freedman, "The Song of the Sea," *Pottery, Poetry, and Prophecy: Studies in Early Hebrew Poetry* (Winona Lake, Indiana: Eisenbrauns, 1980) 179-186; James Muilenburg, "A Liturgy on the Triumphs of Yahweh," *Studia Biblica et Semitica*, Fs. T. C. Vriezen (Wageningen: H. Veenman, 1966): 233-251.

between the vocabulary and concepts of the Song and that of Ugaritic mythology. Moreover, the Song reflects the whole sweep of the Baal myth cycle. The Song belongs to that early period[16].

Objections have been raised to each of the elements of the dating system. There is no agreement that the prosodical features found in the Song are restricted in Hebrew poetry to an early period. Also, it is not clear that we are dealing with mixed meter here, and the strophic structure is no more complex than in many late pieces.

Butler has examined all of the archaic orthography present in the Song and noted that none of it was restricted to an early period in Israelite history; all was in use until the post-exile; so their presence cannot be used as a proof of early dating[17]. The reply of this school would be that individually they may not be restricted to an early period, but the great number of their appearances would indicate the Song's early character. In turn, though, one could answer that they have not given any way of distinguishing the Song from a later composition seeking to be archaic sounding.

Then, while all would concede that they have demonstrated a connection between the Song and the myth system that is also found in Ugaritic literature, the question remains as to whether this indicates early dating? Mowinckel insists that the presence of the myth elements does not argue such. B. Childs notes that the Ugaritic elements are present, but the time of their entrance into Israelite use could as easily be from a late period[18]. Cross himself speaks of the flourishing of myth in Hebrew literature in the period of the exile and post-exile, and

---

16 Cross, "Canaanite Myth" 112-144.
17 Butler, Song 213-237.
18 Brevard S. Childs, *The Book of Exodus*, The Old Testament Library (Philadelphia: Westminster, 1974) 246.

no specific criteria are given to distinguish the myth use of the later period from that of the early period he postulates[19].

Placement with regard to the Pentateuchal sources

There have been various attempts to place the Song within or very close to one of the Pentateuchal traditions. Only Mowinckel ties it to J, seeing in the description of the Sea event the picture drawn not by the Pentateuch as a whole but by that restricted to J[20].

B. Baentsch and W. Staerk maintain that the Deuteronomic spirit is found in the Song. For Tournay the Song is thoroughly Deuteronomic in style and ideology. Butler sees Deuteronomic elements in all the parts of the Song[21]. All of these authors will place the Song in the Deuteronomic epoch. Tournay, Staerk and Butler will specify the end of the monarchy. Foresti places the Song within the Deuteronomistic school of the exile.

Most have noted, rather, that the Song does not fit into any one of the recognized sources. Some of these maintain that it was subsequently incorporated into one or more of the sources. H. Schmidt considers Ex 15:1, 19 to be E, and 15:21 to be J[22]. H. Holzinger, on the other hand, maintains that 15:20, 21 continues 14:31, the E source[23].

Cross and Freedman also maintain that the Song of Miriam has been taken up into E. They then hold that the Song of

---

19 Cross, "Canaanite Myth" 136f.
20 Sigmund Mowinckel, *Psalmenstudien I-II* (1921-24; Amsterdam: P. Schippers, 1961) 2:191.
21 Bruno Baentsch, *Exodus, Leviticus, und Numeri,* Handkommentar zum Alten Testamentum (Gottingen: Vandenhoeck and Ruprecht, 1903) 128-137; Willi W. Staerk, *Die Schriften des Alten Testaments,* vol. 3: *Lyrik* (Gottingen: Vandenhoeck, 1911) 21-23; Butler, Song 247-253.
22 Hans Schmidt, "Das Meerlied. Ex 15:2-19," *Zeitschrift für die alttestamentliche Wissenschaft* 49 (1931): 59-66.
23 Heinrich Holzinger, *Exodus,* Kurzer Hand-Commentar zum Alten Testament (Tubingen: J. C. B. Mohr, 1900) 45-50.

Moses, 15:1-18 has been taken into J. Because J and E both have had the Song enter into their sources, the Song has to antedate both of them. The Song of Miriam is the title of the Song of Moses. And the Song has to have originally been known as the Song of Miriam, because although it is very possible that what was originally a Song of Miriam could be later attributed to Moses, the reverse is not possible[24].

While the line of reasoning of Cross and Freedman could establish the Song as more ancient than the J and E sources, it rests on the assumption that Ex 15:1a and 20, 21a can be identified as either J or E, but M Noth maintains that it is isolated from the narrative sources[25].

Placement within the Reed Sea tradition development

Cross has placed the Song's account of the destruction of the Egyptians before any of the Pentateuchal accounts. What appears in the earliest accounts, the drying of the sea and the entrance of the Israelites, is absent. The Song of the Sea portrays God as the Lord of the storm, v 8. Thus it represents a tradition in which the Egyptians were pursuing the Israelites on barges on the sea and were destroyed in a storm. This is really the earliest account of the Reed Sea event[26].

None has followed Cross in this. The Song of the Sea speaks of horses and chariots pursuing the Israelites, which would have to have been placed on the barges. But there simply is no mention of barges in the Song. Also the picture of destruction by a storm on the sea is contrary to all the other early pictures of the Sea event.

---

24 Cross and Freedman 237-250.
25 Martin Noth, *Exodus*, trans. J. S. Bowden, The Old Testament Library (Philadelphia: Westminster, 1962) 121.
26 Cross, "Canaanite Myth" 131ff.

Holzinger considers that the rendition does not belong to J. He does admit the possibility that P knew the Song because of the use of וְחֵילֹו in 15:4. The Song then pertains to a side source. It was inserted into the Pentateuch after the exile, in the final stages of redaction[27].

Childs has turned his investigations of the development of the Exodus tradition to include the Song of the Sea. He first observes that the Song has some relation to the final text of Ex 14, because the same basic features of wind and wall are present in both. He notes that it cannot be in the line of development of the J source. In the early traditions the Sea event was part of the desert theme, but the Song separates the Sea event from the desert leading theme because there is a shift at v 13 where the leading theme starts. The Song cannot be a very late combination of the J and P sources, because linguistically it does not demonstrate the two sources. It is then a parallel development that grew out of the same wide historical tradition that included J. It is not in the direct line of the development of J to P[28].

Cross finds the Jordan crossing tradition present in v 16b[29]. G. W. Coats sees the Jordan tradition there also, and he finds either a Sea-Conquest or a Sea-River motif present[30].

R. de Vaux first establishes that the motifs of the crossing of the sea and the standing of the waters are not a borrowing by the Jordan River tradition from the Reed Sea tradition. Instead, the flow of these tradition elements is the opposite, from the river to the sea. The standing of the waters of the river is a sober telling of the stoppage of the waters at the time that the

---

27 Holzinger 45-50.
28 Brevard S. Childs, "A tradition-Historical Study of the Reed Sea Tradition," *Vetus Testamentum* 20 (1970): 406-418.
29 Cross, "Canaanite Myth" 141.
30 George W. Coats, "The Song of the Sea," *Catholic Biblical Quarterly* 31 (1969): 1-17.

Israelites first crossed the Jordan. These elements have entered into the later levels of the Reed Sea crossing tradition, only with the miraculous aspect more exaggerated. The original rendition of the Jordan River crossing is described as the water being piled into a נֵד, a heap. Ex 15:8, which uses the same term to describe the standing of the waters of the Sea, is based on the Jordan account and is later[31].

I note that any solution to the problem of where the Song of the Sea stands in the formation of the Reed Sea tradition would have to take certain acquisitions of the critical research into account. The Song has no real relation to the sources present in Ex 14, but it does have a relation to the layout of the final text. If it is a parallel development, where does that development take place? A resolution to the question must also take into account the fact that the Jordan River standing and crossing tradition is present in the Song. The Reed Sea crossing and standing of the waters tradition, which come after the J and E traditions, also have their roots in the Jordan River crossing.

Other traditions present

W. Oesterley and Holzinger maintained that v 12 orginally pertained to the rebellion of Korah story, Nb 16:31-33. J. Watts sees both Ex 15:12b and 6-7 as formerly used for the dramatic telling of the Korah story but now adapted to the story of the sea[32]. That these lines are taken over from the rebellion in the desert story has never won wide acceptance among the critics.

---

31 Roland de Vaux, *The Early History of Israel*, trans. John McHugh, 2 vols. (London: Darton, Longman and Todd, 1978) 1:381-387.

32 W. O. E. Oesterly, *Ancient Hebrew Poems* (London: SPCK, 1938) 18-22; John D. Watts, "The Song of the Sea--Ex. XV," *Vetus Testamentum* 7 (1957): 371-380.

Schreiner considers that the second part of the Song represents a Zion tradition. The phrase "the place for your dwelling" is a statement repeated only in the temple dedication speech of Solomon, 1 Kg 8:13. The term "mountain of your inheritance" is taken over from Canaanite mythology and applied to Zion. This term unites the Zion tradition and the conquest tradition, because it means both God's mountain and the land inherited by the people. The fear that fell on the peoples uses ideas that were part of the tradition of the attack of the nations on the holy city[33].

Oesterley sees Dt-Isaian elements present. He then puts the composition into the exile. Watts posits a long period of composition, but the final form resembles most the Chronicler because it falls into the form of a telling of the mighty acts of God, embracing the sea, the journey in the desert, occupation, and temple.

Historical critical considerations

The notion is that what the Song speaks about can tell us when it was written. The most literal position resulting from this method is that the Song was written by Moses right after the victory at the Reed Sea. S. Garofalo holds for the integral Mosaic composition of the Song. He cites the practice of ancient Near Eastern peoples who improvised songs on the spot on the occasion of victories in war[34].

The objection was raised by Mowinckel that the mention of the land of the Philistines precludes a Mosaic date because the settlement of the Philistines was after that of the Israelites[35]. A reply came from Albright, who wished to place the Song in the

33 Schreiner, *Sion-Jerusalem*.
34 Salvatore Garofalo, "L'Epinicio di Mose," *Biblica* 18 (1937): 1-22.
35 Sigmund Mowinckel, *Der Achtundsechzigste Psalm* (Oslo: 1953) 74.

13th century. He tried to push the arrival of the Philistines behind the twelfth, but this attempt has not achieved acceptance[36]. Another objection to the Mosaic dating has been the description of the conquest and the setting up of the sanctuary. Garofalo sought a resolution by maintaining that the sanctuary is the whole land. Watts has embraced the same position.

Others holding for a pre-monarchic origin have maintained that the sanctuary is Shiloh (H. Ewald), the desert shrine (Freedman), or Shittim as the place of arrival and any Yahwistic shrine as the sanctuary (Cross)[37].

Cross and Freedman note the use of chiefs of Edom and princes of Moab in the Song. Thus, they place it in the period before their monarchies were established. The mention of the Philistines makes it not earlier than the twelfth century and the lack of monarchies means that it cannot be later than the eleventh[38]. W. Baudissin, on the other hand, held that a fear-conquest tradition that presents Philistia, Edom, and Moab as terror stricken would have to be far removed from the actual events[39].

The reading of v 17 as reference to the Jerusalem sanctuary often goes hand in hand with dating the psalm within the Deuteronomic era (Rylaarsdam, Baentsch), usually to the end of the monarchy (Butler), and more specifically to the Passover of Josiah (Tournay, Staerk).

R. Pfeiffer maintains that the Song is thinking of the completed second temple, and was written in the second half of the fifth century[40].

---

36 Cross, "Canaanite Myth" 124, note 39.
37 Freedman, "Early Israelite History" 141; Cross, "Canaanite Myth" 138ff.
38 Cross and Freedman 237-250.
39 Wolf Wilhelm Baudissin, *Einleitung in die Bucher des Alten Testamentes* (Liepzig: S. Hirzel, 1901) 95f.
40 Robert H. Pfeiffer, *Introduction to the Old Testament* (New York: Harper, 1941) 274.

Holzinger, who places the Song in the post-exile, sees the return from the exile present in the account of the return from Egypt.

Compilation

A strong unity of composition has been maintained by Cross and Freedman, Baentsch, Mowinckel, Coats, Holzinger, and Tournay, though Cross and Freedman allow that v 2 was added when the Song was adapted to temple use. George Adam Smith held that vv 1b-12 were of Mosaic authorship. Vv 13-18 had to have been after the conquest; therefore he maintained two periods of authorship[41]. Muilenburg also considers vv 1-12 and 13-18 to be of two different periods of composition. Staerk, Noth, Watts, and Strauss hold for a development into the final form of the Song. A very large number of critics consider "The Song of Miriam," v 21b, to have existed separately at one time (Noth, de Vaux, Tournay, Baentsch, Holzinger, Cornill, Schmidt). Those who separate this verse always hold that it is more ancient than the Song of Moses, vv 1-18. It is often held to be the oldest of all the renditions of the Reed Sea story (de Vaux, Noth).

This position was strongly criticized by Mowinckel. He noted that earlier dating of the so called "Song of Miriam" rests only on the notion that a short vibrant piece of poetry is earlier. This is based on a fully ungrounded schematic of literary and religious evolution[42]. He maintained that v 21 was taken from the hymn and never had an independent existence.

---

41 George Adam Smith, *The Early Poetry of Israel in its Physical and Social Origins* (London: Oxford, 1912) 51.
42 Mowinckel, *Psalmenstudien* 2:111f note 4.

Cultic nature of the Song

Most hold that the hymn was for use at the Passover. They rely on the subject matter of the Song, the passing over the Sea. Others consider it a victory song (Cross and Freedman, Albright, Garofalo, de Vaux). The two notions are not necessarily mutually exclusive. Cross considers it a victory hymn but places its cultic transmission at the Passover festival at Gilgal[43]. A few place it in the autumn festival, normally on the strength of v 18. The acclamation of Yahweh's kingship is sure sign for Mowinckel that the Song belongs within the enthronement festival. Schmidt places it within the ambit of the thanksgiving psalms.

Authorship

Tournay has suggested that because of the emphasis on holiness--קֹדֶשׁ appears three times, vv 11, 13, 17--the author is either a priest or a Levite.

Prosody

There is simply no agreement on the strophic arrangement. The most extensive work has been done by Freedman[44] and Muilenburg. The metrical pattern in all modern studies resolves to a basic 2+2 pattern with some entrance of 3+3.

---

43 Cross, "Canaanite Myth" 141f.
44 David Noel Freedman, "Strophe and Meter in Exodus 15," *Pottery, Poetry, and Prophecy: Studies in Early Hebrew Poetry* (Winona Lake, Indiana: Eisenbrauns, 1980) 187-228.

Statement of the Argument

The thesis

The position set forth in this work is that the Song of the Sea is a unified composition wholly the product of Levitical cult personnel of the second temple. It has a processional entrance form and was written sometime after the completion of the walls of Jerusalem by Nehemiah. The specific authorship of the psalmic section comes from within the clan of the Sons of Asaph. The prose framework was written by Levitical teachers who were also leaders in arrangements for the cult. The prose framework and the Song were written in one unified project, and both were created with the express intention of placing the Song after Ex 14, and for the purpose of adapting the exodus account for use in the liturgy

Elements of the previous research enter into the treatment, but this work seeks to explain the whole scope of acquisitions exposed therein. Virtually everything gained in the research will enter into the discussion. The Song of the Sea demonstrates late vocabulary and usages. The Baal myth is present in the whole sweep of the Song. There is an intense use of archaic orthography. It has a general relation to confessional forms. It is also has ties to the long historical resumes.

The Song does not fall within any of the Pentateuchal sources, neither in the Song, nor in the framework. But the formulation of the Reed Sea event shows some relation to the JE and P traditions found in Ex 14. Also, the sweep of events is not independent of the formulation of Ex 14. The text shows the intense presence of D elements in all of its parts.

The God of the storm motif is present in v 8. The Jordan River crossing tradition is present in vv 8, 16b. A Sea-Conquest theology has influenced the Song. The passing of the Israelites and the standing of the waters begin as tradition elements in the story of the crossing of the Jordan, from there it arrives at the P version of the Reed Sea crossing. The formulation found in the Song to describe the standing of the waters of the Reed Sea ultimately depends on the Jordan River standing tradition.

The formulation of v 12b could relate to the story of Korah and Dathan's rebellion in the desert. The rendition of the fear of the peoples upon the arrival and conquest of the Israelites is distant from the event because it is at variance with the early traditions. Dt-Isaian elements are present in the Song. The return from the exile has influenced the formulation of the arrival at the holy land.

The description of the sanctuary of v 17 uses Ugaritic myth forms to express a Zion tradition, and it certainly refers to the temple, but in such a way that the rest of the land is not excluded. The fear of the peoples has only an indirect relationship to the conspiracy of the nations and the inviolability of the city traditions.

Authorship is from the Levites who are very concerned with temple traditions. V 18 is to be placed within the tradition stream of Yahweh's rule from Jerusalem and the temple, which emanates from Dt-Is.

In its overall structure and in all of its parts the Song demonstrates an extremely strong unity of composition. The "Song of Miriam" is the first line of the Song, formulated now as an invitation to praise so that it is suitable for use as a refrain. It has never existed independently from the Song. The composers wished to present the hearer with a victory song, and it was composed for the Passover feast.

Lexicographical treatment will enter wherever there is some pattern of use in a period. Words of very frequent occurrence or words whose appearances do not reveal any pattern are not necessarily examined. Usages or specific applications of a word, especially when they reveal themselves as part of a theological development, are investigated. Any word pair that falls into a pattern identifiable with what is found in the Song is mentioned and analyzed.

All instances of phrasing occurring elsewhere are noted and treated. By phrasing I mean three words or more that coincide with phrasing in the Song, or a congruence of words and poetic form that are close enough so that a definite relation to phrasing in the Song can be claimed. Wherever possible, evidence for the line of dependence is given. Also, the study of individual word forms that have a clear coincidence with those in the Song are noted.

By the conjunction of the above elements, vocabulary, usages, phrasing, and forms, I seek to establish that the Song belonged to a period of style that existed only in the second temple, and that flourished around the period of Nehemiah.

I trace the development of tradition in all the parts of the Song. Myth elements are noted, and the period when they were used and then developed in Israel is treated. Historical indicators within the Song are then employed to place it during the time of friction between Israel and her neighbors and after the re-building of the walls in the face of their opposition.

CHAPTER TWO
PRELIMINARY QUESTIONS

The Text

The entire text under consideration is Ex 15:1-21. It contains a psalm, vv 1b-18, 21b, and a prose framework, vv 1a, 19-21a.

The psalm can be divided into three sections. There is a formulaic liturgical enclosure, vv 1b-3, 18, 21b. The rest of the Song is divided into two parts: part one comprises vv 4-12 and is a description of the sea event; part two, vv 13-17, is a telling of the entrance into Canaan.

Within the prose framework there are liturgical rubrics for the performance of the psalm, vv 1a, 20, 21a, and a quasi-poetic explanation of the psalm, v 19.

Ex 15:1-21

1a	אָז יָשִׁיר־מֹשֶׁה וּבְנֵי יִשְׂרָאֵל אֶת־הַשִּׁירָה הַזֹּאת לַיהוָֹה וַיֹּאמְרוּ לֵאמֹר
1b	אָשִׁירָה לַיהוָֹה כִּי־גָאֹה גָּאָה סוּס וְרֹכְבוֹ רָמָה בַיָּם:
2a	עָזִּי וְזִמְרָת יָהּ וַיְהִי־לִי לִישׁוּעָה:
2b	זֶה אֵלִי וְאַנְוֵהוּ אֱלֹהֵי אָבִי וַאֲרֹמְמֶנְהוּ
3	יְהוָה אִישׁ מִלְחָמָה יְהוָה שְׁמוֹ:
4a	מַרְכְּבֹת פַּרְעֹה וְחֵילוֹ יָרָה בַיָּם
4b	וּמִבְחַר שָׁלִשָׁיו טֻבְּעוּ בְיַם־סוּף:
5	תְּהֹמֹת יְכַסְיֻמוּ יָרְדוּ בִמְצוֹלֹת כְּמוֹ־אָבֶן:
6	יְמִינְךָ יְהוָה נֶאְדָּרִי בַּכֹּחַ יְמִינְךָ יְהוָה תִּרְעַץ אוֹיֵב:
7	וּבְרֹב גְּאוֹנְךָ תַּהֲרֹס קָמֶיךָ תְּשַׁלַּח חֲרֹנְךָ יֹאכְלֵמוֹ כַּקַּשׁ:
8a	וּבְרוּחַ אַפֶּיךָ נֶעֶרְמוּ מַיִם נִצְּבוּ כְמוֹ־נֵד נֹזְלִים

8b   קָפְא֥וּ תְהֹמֹ֖ת בְּלֶב־יָֽם׃

9a   אָמַ֥ר אוֹיֵ֛ב אֶרְדֹּ֥ף אַשִּׂ֖יג אֲחַלֵּ֣ק שָׁלָ֑ל

9b   תִּמְלָאֵ֣מוֹ נַפְשִׁ֔י אָרִ֣יק חַרְבִּ֔י תּוֹרִישֵׁ֖מוֹ יָדִֽי׃

10   נָשַׁ֥פְתָּ בְרוּחֲךָ֖ כִּסָּ֣מוֹ יָ֑ם צָֽלֲלוּ֙ כַּֽעוֹפֶ֔רֶת בְּמַ֖יִם אַדִּירִֽים׃

11a   מִֽי־כָמֹ֤כָה בָּֽאֵלִם֙ יְהֹוָ֔ה מִ֥י כָּמֹ֖כָה נֶאְדָּ֣ר בַּקֹּ֑דֶשׁ

11b   נוֹרָ֥א תְהִלֹּ֖ת עֹ֥שֵׂה פֶֽלֶא׃

12   נָטִ֙יתָ֙ יְמִ֣ינְךָ֔ תִּבְלָעֵ֖מוֹ אָֽרֶץ׃

13   נָחִ֥יתָ בְחַסְדְּךָ֖ עַם־ז֣וּ גָּאָ֑לְתָּ נֵהַ֥לְתָּ בְעָזְּךָ֖ אֶל־נְוֵ֥ה קָדְשֶֽׁךָ׃

14   שָֽׁמְע֥וּ עַמִּ֖ים יִרְגָּז֑וּן חִ֣יל אָחַ֔ז יֹשְׁבֵ֖י פְּלָֽשֶׁת׃

15a   אָ֤ז נִבְהֲלוּ֙ אַלּוּפֵ֣י אֱד֔וֹם אֵילֵ֣י מוֹאָ֔ב יֹֽאחֲזֵ֖מוֹ רָ֑עַד

15b   נָמֹ֕גוּ כֹּ֖ל יֹשְׁבֵ֥י כְנָֽעַן׃

16a   תִּפֹּ֨ל עֲלֵיהֶ֤ם אֵימָ֙תָה֙ וָפַ֔חַד בִּגְדֹ֥ל זְרוֹעֲךָ֖ יִדְּמ֣וּ כָּאָ֑בֶן

16b   עַד־יַעֲבֹ֤ר עַמְּךָ֙ יְהֹוָ֔ה עַֽד־יַעֲבֹ֖ר עַם־ז֥וּ קָנִֽיתָ׃

17a   תְּבִאֵ֗מוֹ וְתִטָּעֵ֙מוֹ֙ בְּהַ֣ר נַחֲלָֽתְךָ֔ מָכ֧וֹן לְשִׁבְתְּךָ֛ פָּעַ֖לְתָּ יְהֹוָ֑ה

17b   מִקְּדָ֕שׁ אֲדֹנָ֖י כּוֹנְנ֥וּ יָדֶֽיךָ׃

18   יְהֹוָ֥ה ׀ יִמְלֹ֖ךְ לְעֹלָ֥ם וָעֶֽד׃

19   כִּ֣י בָא֩ ס֨וּס פַּרְעֹ֜ה בְּרִכְבּ֤וֹ וּבְפָרָשָׁיו֙ בַּיָּ֔ם וַיָּ֧שֶׁב יְהֹוָ֛ה עֲלֵהֶ֖ם אֶת־מֵ֣י הַיָּ֑ם וּבְנֵ֧י יִשְׂרָאֵ֛ל הָלְכ֥וּ בַיַּבָּשָׁ֖ה בְּת֥וֹךְ הַיָּֽם׃

20a   וַתִּקַּח֩ מִרְיָ֨ם הַנְּבִיאָ֜ה אֲח֧וֹת אַהֲרֹ֛ן אֶת־הַתֹּ֖ף בְּיָדָ֑הּ

20b   וַתֵּצֶ֤אןָ כָֽל־הַנָּשִׁים֙ אַחֲרֶ֔יהָ בְּתֻפִּ֖ים וּבִמְחֹלֹֽת׃

21a   וַתַּ֥עַן לָהֶ֖ם מִרְיָ֑ם

21b   שִׁ֤ירוּ לַֽיהֹוָה֙ כִּֽי־גָאֹ֣ה גָּאָ֔ה ס֥וּס וְרֹכְב֖וֹ רָמָ֥ה בַיָּֽם׃

1a   Then Moses and the Sons of Israel sang this song to Yahweh, and they said:

1b   I will sing to the Lord for he is highly exalted, horse and rider he has thrown into the sea.

2a   My strength and my song is Yah, and he has been my saviour.

2b   This is my El and I will praise him, the God of my father and I will exalt him.

3   Yahweh is a man of war; Yahweh is his name.

4   Pharaoh's chariots and army he has cast into the sea, and his choice officers have sunk into the Reed Sea.

5   The abyss covered them; they went down into the depths like a stone.

6   Your right hand, Yahweh, is glorious in power; your right hand, Yahweh, smashes the enemy.

7   By the greatness of your majesty you overturn your adversaries; you send forth your fury; it consumes them like straw.

8   By the breath of your nostrils the waters pile up; the streams stand up like a dike; the depths solidified in the heart of the sea.

9   The enemy says, "I will pursue, I will overtake, I will share out the spoil, my soul will be satiated, I will draw out my sword, my hand will dispossess them."

10   You blew with your breath, the sea covered them, they sank like lead into the mighty waters.

11   Who is like you among the gods, Yahweh, who is like you magnificent in holiness, awesome in praiseworthy deeds, doer of wonders?

12   You stretched out your right hand, the earth swallowed them.

13   In your constancy you led the people you had redeemed, in your strength you guided them to your holy resting place.

14   The peoples hear and tremble, pangs seize the dwellers of Philistia.

15   Then the chieftains of Edom are dismayed, the great ones of Moab are seized with terror, all the dwellers of Canaan melt with fear.

16   Terror and dread fall on them; in the greatness of your arm they are still as a stone,

16b until your people pass over, Yahweh, until the people you purchased pass over.

17 You bring them in and plant them on the mountain of your inheritance, your dwelling place which you have made, the sanctuary of the Lord which your hands have established.

18 Yahweh will reign for ever and ever!

19a For Pharaoh's horses, chariots and charioteers went into the sea, and Yahweh brought back on them the waters of the sea,

19b and the Sons of Israel went on dry land in the midst of the sea.

20a And Miriam the prophetess, the sister of Aaron, took a tambourine in her hand,

20b while all the women went out after her with tambourines dancing,

21a and Miriam sang a refrain to them:

21b Sing to the Lord for he is highly exalted, horse and rider he has thrown into the sea.

Notes

V 2a, for זִמְרָת the Greek has σκεπαστής, my hiding place, see Dt 32:38.

V 3a, for אִישׁ the targums and the Syriac have גִּבּוֹר, under the influence, no doubt, of Ps 24:8. The Greek has συντρίβων.

V 11, for בַּקֹּדֶשׁ, the Greek has ἐν ἁγίοις, among the holy ones, which maintains a parallelism with the אֵלִם, the gods, of 11a.

Perfectly preserved, the text shows no corruptions or evidence of displacements. The variants in the versions are few, and never sufficient to emend the text.

The Unity and Poetic Technique of the Song, vv 1b-18, 21b

The formulaic enclosure, vv 1b-3, 18, 21b

This section is dominated by high confessional praise of Yahweh the warrior. In vv 1b, 2, the psalmist speaks in the first person, something that does not return for the rest of the work. These verses are followed by v 3, which has a doxological form and should, therefore, have the function of concluding and closing off the preceding praise material; see Am 5:8; 9:6, also 4:13; 5:27; Is 47:4; 48:2; Jer 46:18; 48:15; 51:57, etc.

The whole introductory section, vv 1b-3, refers to God in the third person. This motif continues into v 5. V 6 addresses God in the second person. The direct address form continues through v 17. In v 18 there is a reversion to the third person, which is then also found in the responsorial refrain, v 21b. Also, v 18 has the same form as v 3, Yahweh's name as declamatory introduces each discrete acclamatory phrase in both verses.

All of the verses involved, vv 1-3, 18, 21b, are of standard liturgical form, and except for v 1bβ, which describes the specific action of God against the enemy cavalry, they are composed of highly generalized praise language. Thus, these verses can be seen as a liturgical introduction and conclusion to establish the cult form of the Song.

The introductory section, though it evidences differences in style from part one, cannot be separated from it. It sets the whole tone for the rest of the section, praise that celebrates God the warrior. V 3 has the form of a concluding doxology. Therefore, it has its natural use as concluding the previous verses and cannot be postulated as beginning the Song. It then introduces the enactment of the victory of God the warrior over the forces of Pharaoh, v 4. Also, v 4 states that "he" threw

Pharaoh's chariots into the sea. Without the preceding verses, the "he" would have no referent. Thus, v 4 cannot begin the Song. It can be concluded that all of vv 1-3 are integral to the composition of vv 1-12 of the Song.

It can also be mentioned that, though linguistically tied to vv 1b-3, the affirmation of the kingly rule of Yahweh in v 18 stands well in its present position after the second part; because the statement of the kingship of Yahweh theme, where Yahweh the king leads the people into the sanctuary, vv 13-17, is very widely used in psalmic and other literature. See Ps 24:7-10; 48:3, 13-15; 68:25; 84:2-4; 95:1-3; 96:7-10, 13 = 1 Chr 16:28-31, 33b; 98:6, 9; Mic 2:13; 4:6f.

Part one, vv 4-12

This section speaks in high praise language with mythopoetic overtones of God's defeat of the Egyptians at the Reed Sea. Within part one there is an interlude where the action of God on the waters is suddenly broken by a descent into the mind of the enemy and portrays his intention to continue his pursuit into the waters, v 9. This cannot be considered an addition. V 10a speaks of the waters covering "them." The "them" refers to the enemies to whose decision we have been privy in the preceding verse.

Vv 1b-12, 18, 21b treated as a unit

The whole of the liturgical enclosure and part one demonstrates a thematic and linguistic unity. The sections are dominated by water terms, the most used being יָם, sea, vv 1bβ, 21bβ, 4ab, 8b, 10a. Then מַיִם, waters, is found in vv 8a, 10b, נֹזְלִים, streams, in v 8a. The water terms can have a mythical quality, תְּהֹמֹת, abyss, vv 5a, 8b, מְצוֹלֹת, depths, v 5b.

Further linguistic unity is shown by the repetitious use of praise words: אַדִּר, majestic, in vv 6a, 11aβ, of God, in v 10b, of the waters; גֵּאֶה, glorious, in vv 1ba bis, 21ba bis, 7a. Other repetitions that are found: אֵל, God, v 2b; אֱלִם, gods, v 11a; כסה, cover, vv 5, 10; רוּחַ, wind, vv 8, 10; יָמִין, right hand, vv 6ab, 12; אוֹיֵב, enemy, vv 6b, 9a.

Poetic technique in vv 1b-12, 18, 21b

In terms of poetic style the whole first section is marked by intense parallelism. Parallelism within the same strophe is found in vv 2baβ, 4ab, 5ab, 7ab, 8aaβb. And there is connective parallelism between verses, vv 1bβ is substantially repeated in 4a; 5 reappears in 10aβb.

In v 2b there is the repetition of five words beginning with א, which appears again in v 9a. There are further similarities that establish a very strong unity of style between vv 2 and 9. They both use marked patterns of sound plays with consonants and vowels. V 2 emphasizes the *hīrek* sound as part of its prosodical technique. It intersperses it with other very tightly connected sound rhymes. 2aaβbaβ have the following patterns:

$$
\begin{array}{ll}
\text{עָזִּי וְזִמְרָת יָהּ} & 2aa \\
\text{הָ} \quad \text{זִ} \quad \text{זִ} & \\
\text{וַיְהִי־לִי לִישׁוּעָה} & \beta \\
\text{הָ} \quad \text{הִי לִי לִי} & \\
\text{אֵל} \quad \text{יְ} \quad \text{וַאֲ...הוּ} & 2ba \\
\text{אֱל} \quad \text{...יְ} \quad \text{וַאֲ...הוּ} & \beta
\end{array}
$$

Very similar phenomena can be seen in 9b. The line is dominated by the *hīrek* sound, interspersed with תּ... מוֹ, to give this tight pattern: תּ... מוֹ ... תּ... ... יְ ... ... יְ ... ... יְ ... תּ... מוֹ ... יְ

The poet also likes to use intense repetition as a stylistic device, especially in the initiating element of verses. יהוה in v 3a, repeated in 3b, then introduces the laudatory phrasing again in v 18. Similarly, in vv 6, 11 the beginning word pair is repeated in the second hemistich. This type of stylistic flourish also appears connecting vv 7 and 8, where each verse begins with וּבְר... ךְ.

We can conclude that there are very strong indications of compact unity that embrace all of the interior enclosure and the first part.

Poetic technique in part two, vv 13-17

There is a looser cohesion in the second part in accordance with the generally more expansive pastoral tone found there. Still, we can demonstrate its interior unity. There is the sense of one ongoing movement that begins with God leading and guiding his people in v 13, continues with his people passing over, v 16b, and ends with his bringing his people in and planting them in the sanctuary, v 17.

The movement is interrupted in vv 14-16a, where the Song speaks of the fear of the various peoples, but these verses are integral to the composition of the second part. V 16b has a clear linguistic connection with v 13, both use the expression "people whom" containing the unusual archaic form זו. But v 16b, though linguistically tied to v 13, cannot logically follow. The expression "until your people pass" makes no sense when placed next to v 13b, "You led them to your sacred pasture." It has to have the mention of the peoples who fear, vv 14-16a, "until your people pass." Thus, all of vv 13-16 is coherent and in place. Then v 17 naturally continues the movement to its term, the sanctuary.

There are also linguistic indications of unity. עַם, people, appears in vv 13, and 16baβ to indicate the people of God, and is contrasted to the peoples, v 14. יֹשְׁבֵי, dwellers, appears in vv 14, 15, to represent the foreign inhabitants of Canaan and the surrounding areas; it is contrasted with Yahweh, the true dweller of the sacred area, v 17ab. Then קֹדֶשׁ, holy, v 13, is repeated in the cognate word, מִקְדָשׁ, sanctuary, v 17b.

The poetic style of part two is, like the rest of the Song, marked by parallelism within the same strophe, vv 13ab; 16baβ; 17aβb. Or the parallelism can run through strophes, specifically the compilation of equivalent terms running through vv 14-16a. Thus, see 14ab, 15aaβb, 16aaβ Also, the same technique of interior repetition that likes to repeat the initiating phrase, that we found in part one, appears in part two. The sound pattern, נָ...תָ...בְ...ךָ, beginning 13a also begins 13b. The first three words of 16ba are repeated in 16bβ. The form תִ..מוֹ in the first word of v 17 is duplicated in the next word.

Overall unity of the Song and its poetic technique

There is a difference of theme and tone between part two and the rest of the Song; therefore, the points of verbal contact are not numerous; the following, though, appear. The root קֹדֶשׁ is found vv 11, 13, 17, כְּאָבֶן, like a stone, in vv 5, 16, עֹז, strength, vv 2, 13, יָד, hand, 9b, 17b. Despite the relatively sparse verbal agreement, part two should be held to be of one composition with the rest of the Song. There is striking agreement in style, enough to demonstrate with certainty that all of the Song falls within one authorship and was written in one period.

Already mentioned is the intense parallelism that embraces all of the sections of the Song. Also, the author likes to elongate the normal bistich form to additional elements, as if to strengthen his point by the accumulation of terms. This technique is found vv 8, 9, 11, 15, 17.

There is the same technique of repetition of initial elements. Also the pattern מוֹ...תָ repeated in v 17aα as a poetic flourish within the verse, was also repeated for poetic style in v 9b.

Furthermore, the text does not lend itself to division. The only place where there is a change of tone and theme is after v 12. Up till then there is the depiction of God's defeat of the Egyptians by the waters. The language is dynamic and filled with tension. From v 13 on the Song speaks of the leading and entering theme and has a sense of ease and security. But in terms of the poetic structure, vv 12 and 13 hinge together as well as anything in the poem. The initial phrases of vv 12, 13ab, have a very strong character of assonance and consonance, which between vv 12 and 13a is extreme:

$$
\begin{array}{ll}
\text{...ךָ יְמִין יִֽ תָ יט נָ} & 12a \\
\text{...ךָ בְחַסְ תָ י חָ נָ} & 13aα \\
\text{...ךָ בְעָזְ תָ לְ הַ נָ} & 13bα
\end{array}
$$

This same rhyming scheme appears also in v 10aα, נָשַׁפְתָ בְרוּחֲךָ. All of the phrases have the sense of God carrying out his deliverance by means of a quasi-personified attribute.

The author likes to depict these quasi-personified attributes of God in the form בְ...ךָ. See בְרוּחַ אַפֶּיךָ, 7a; בְרֹב גְאוֹנְךָ, 8a; בְרוּחֲךָ, 10a; בְחַסְדְךָ, 13a; בְעָזְךָ13b; בִּגְדֹל זְרוֹעֲךָ, 16aβ. See also בְּהַר נַחֲלָתְךָ, 17aα, his mountain, which has a quasi-identification with God.

The composer is fond of sound rhymes in general. The anomalous form אַנְוֵהוּ, 2bα, probably has its formulation for its sound value and is a conscious correlation to נָוֵה in v 13bβ.

Both parts contain an interlude which break the action but is part of the integral composition, vv 9, 14-16a. Each is a departure to depict the mental state of the other peoples. The interludes themselves have the same character of piling up terms in a staccato manner. Each is enclosed by verses that contain a key term that links them and continues the flow of the action. "Your breath," רוּחַ, links the action of vv 8 and 10, where God destroys the Egyptians by means of the waters. "Your people" holds together vv 13 and 16b and allows for the continuity of the action of God leading his people. The coordination of style is of great subtlety and delicacy. Such an agreement of minute elements of poetic technique is too much to ask of a redactor of a different period.

There are three verses that are acclamations, two in the first part, vv 6, 11, and one in the second part, v 16b. They all have the following essential form: a/Yahweh in the vocative/b; a/c.

$$c \,/\, \text{voc} \,/\, a \,; \qquad\qquad b \,/\, \text{voc} \,/\, a$$
6   יְמִינְךָ / יהוה / נֶאְדָּרִי בַּכֹּחַ ; יְמִינְךָ / יהוה / תִּרְעַץ אוֹיֵב

$$c \,/\qquad\quad a \,; \;\; \text{voc} \,/\quad b \,/\qquad\quad a$$
11a   מִי־כָמֹכָה / בָּאֵלִם / יהוה ; מִי כָּמֹכָה / נֶאְדָּר בַּקֹּדֶשׁ

$$c \,/\quad b \,/\qquad\quad a \,; \;\; \text{voc} \,/\quad b \,/\qquad\quad a$$
16b   עַד־יַעֲבֹר / עַמְּךָ / יהוה ; עַד־יַעֲבֹר / עַם־זוּ / קָנִיתָ

There are slight variations, but that does not destroy the fact that they are basically the same acclamatory form. And each of these verses has been shown to be integral to its respective part. Then, all of the acclamations are preceded by a statement of the total helplessness of the adversary. Vv 5 and 16a have the same expression, כְּמוֹ־אָבֶן and כָּאָבֶן, like a stone, and v 10 has the equivalent expression כַּעוֹפֶרֶת, like lead.

The Song uses the imperfect in reference to past events, and it changes from the imperfect to the perfect in the same sentence, even though it is clear that it means to stay in the same time frame. The phenomenon is found elsewhere, especially in psalmic literature, but the frequency and pervasiveness of use in the Song can be classified as a stylistic trait, and it runs through both parts, vv 5a, 7ab$a\beta$, 12b, 15aβ, 16aaβbaβ, 17aa bis.

Of great importance is the use of the archaic pronominal suffix מוֹ. In the Scripture this particle can come either after a noun or a verb--leaving aside for the moment the more common form after a preposition. But in the Song it always appears as a verbal suffix. מוֹ as a verbal suffix appears 23 times in all the Scripture, and the Song contains nine of them. The highest elsewhere is two. It is obvious that it is intentional and artificial, both because of the high number of appearances and because it cannot be just coincidence that it always appears here after verb forms. If it were just the natural use of an ancient form, it would appear indifferently after both nouns and verbs.

Now this form appears with proportionate frequency in both parts of the Song, vv 5a, 7b, 9baβ, 10a, 12b, 15aβ, 17aa bis. The fact that this trait runs throughout the Song is incompatible with the notion that a later redactor added part two. One would have to posit a redactor that was careful to include into his addition the archaic endings, which is much to ask of a redactor. And then he would have to realize that only archaic endings after verbs would be truly consonant with the work to which he was adding. The existence of such a redactor is not a reasonable hypothesis. This trait is a very strong motive for holding for unity of composition of the entire Song.

The use of מוֹ endings is part of a wider technique in which the author uses high poetic forms as part his style. The מוֹ form is also present in כְּמוֹ, vv 5, 8. I note the final morpheme ־ִי, in נֶאְדָּרִי, v 6, final ן in יְרַגְּזוּן, v 14, and in אֵימָתָה, v 16a, the accusative of intention.

Such forms can also be archaic. אֱרֹמְמֶנְהוּ, v 2b, represents an uncontracted suffix form. There is the returned י of the ל״ה verb, יְכַסְיֻמוּ, 5a. זוּ, vv 13a, 16bβ, is considered a more primitive form of the relative pronoun. This system of poetic flourishes runs indifferently through the enclosure and parts one and two. Thus, there is conclusive evidence from structure, style, grammatical usage, and archaic forms that there is an overall compositional unity to the Song of the Sea.

A note on the archaic character of the text

On the strength of the above data on archaic language some authors have concluded to a very early date for the Song. The first thing that can be noted, though, is that the appearance of the מוֹ ending within the Old Testament shows no pattern of usage in archaic pieces. Many of its appearances are late, extending into the post-exile. Moreover, the multiple occurrences of this ending has nothing to do with dating; it is a matter of literary type. In every instance where you have more than one occurrence following nouns and/or verbs, the passage is a description of God's action of vengeance against the enemy or the ungodly, or the psalmist is asking God to take such an action against them, or it is a description of the actions of the ungodly; that is, it falls within the general category of imprecation literature. The occurrences are Dt 32:27, 32, 37, 38; Ps 2:3ab, 5; 17:10ab; 21:10, 11, 13; 58:7 bis; 59:12 bis, 13 bis, 14; 73:5, 6, 7; 83:12a bis, 12b, 14; 140:4, 10 bis[1]. In some of these instances the device is complemented by the use of the ending after the preposition, see Ps 2:4, 5; 58:5 bis, 8 three times, 9, 10 bis; 73:6, 10, 18. See also Ps 80:6 followed by an appearance with

---

1　E. Kautzsch, *Gesenius' Hebrew Grammar*, trans. A. E. Cowley, 2nd ed. (Oxford: Clarendon, 1910) par 58 g, 91 l.

the preposition, v 7, which is a description of the enemy. Most of the instances of a single occurrence also have the same character, Ex 23:31; Dt 33:29; Ps 5:11; 35:16; 49:12; Jb 27:23.

The multiple use is obviously a stylistic device. It is also clear that the Song belongs to this type of literature. There is the description of God's actions against the Egyptians and the surrounding peoples, and the descent into the way they think. So it is a matter of intentional style and artificial. The artificial use of these forms would favor an author of a later period who intentionally used archaisms rather than a truly ancient author.

The usage of the other archaic grammatical forms extends into the post-exilic period, and the pattern of their appearances does not even favor an early period[2].

We note also that the exact form of the acclamations in vv 6, 11, 16b already appears in Ugaritic poetry from the fourteenth century, see KTU: 1.2, IV, 8f. The Ugaritic text has the same basic sequencing, a/b/Baal in vocative/; a/b/c, discussed above. Compare:

1.2, IV, 8f   Now you will smite your enemy, O Baal,
               now you will smite your enemy,
               now you must cut off your adversary.

28f   Scatter him, O mightiest Baal!
               Scatter him, O rider on the clouds!

Ex 15:6   Your right hand, O Yahweh, is raised in might,
               your right hand, O Yahweh, will smite the enemy.

---

2 The suffix מו is found in Jer 5:22; 22:24; Ps 72:15; Dt 32:10 bis; see Kautzsch par 58 k; Butler 223. Returned ּי: Nb 24:6; Dt 8:13; 32:37; Is 16:9; 17:12; 21:12; 25:6; 26:11; 31:3; 33:7; 40:18, 25; 41:5; 46:5; Ps 36:8, 9; 39:7; 57:2; 73:2; 77:4; 78:44; 83:3; 122:6; Prov 26:7; Jb 3:25; 12:6; 16:22; 19:2; 30:14; Kautzsch par 75 u, v, x, dd, gg. וֹ: Is 42:24; 43:21; Hab 1:11; Ps 9:16; 10:2; 12:8; 17:9; 32:8; 62:12; 68:29; 142:4; 143:8.

But here also the usage in Scripture does not favor an early period. The form appears in Is 26:15; Ps 17:14; 77:17; 89:52; 92:10; 93:3. Of these Is 26; Ps 77; 89; 92, are late[3]. The critical opinion regarding Ps 93 is divided[4]. In regard to Ps 17 it must be noted that the text is corrupt and has certainly been retouched[5]. Moreover, Ps 92:10 is virtually a composite quotation from the above cited Ugaritic texts:

Ps 92:10   For, behold, your enemies, O Yahweh,
              For, behold, your enemies will perish,
              All doers of evil will be scattered.

And the widely held opinion concerning Ps 92 is that it is of the second temple[6].

Nor can the multiplication of archaic elements be of value for establishing an early period of composition. We have already seen that the ending מוֹ appears a very large number of times, and that it is intentional. It can be presumed that the multiplication of archaic elements is also intentional, and part of the style. In fact, once it is concluded that this phenomenon is artificial, a late dating is the more likely inference.

The Form: A Victory Song

Indications in the framework

At least the composers of the framework treated it as a victory song. It was the practice in Israel from ancient times for

3   For the discussion on Ps 77 and 89 see pp 116-120 below.
4   Gianfranco Ravasi, *Il Libro dei Salmi: Commento e Attualizzazione*, 3 vols. (Bologna: Dehoniane, 1981-84) 2:942-44.
5   K. Elliger and W. Rudolph, eds., *Biblica Hebraica Stuttgartensia* (Stuttgart: Deutsche Bibelstiftung, 1966-77) note a to Ps 17:14.
6   Ravasi 2:921f; A. F. Kirkpatrick, *The Book of Psalms* (1902; Grand Rapids: Baker, 1982) 558f.

the women to go out with dance and timbrels to sing a refrain to the men returning after a victory. Compare 21f with the victory songs to David, 1 Sm 18:6; 21:12; 29:5, and Jephthah, Jg 11:34:

vv 20,21	Sm 18:6, 7	Jg 11:34
תֵּצֶאןָ	תֵּצֶאנָה	יֹצֵאת
כָל הַנָּשִׁים	הַנָּשִׁים מִכָּל	
בְּתֻפִּים	בְּתֻפִּים	בְּתֻפִּים
וּבִמְחֹלֹת	וְהַמְּחֹלוֹת	וּבִמְחֹלוֹת
שִׁירוּ	לָשִׁיר	
וַתַּעַן	וַתַּעֲנֶינָה	
refrain follows	refrain follows	

Also the arrangement for the victory song of Judith, Jdt 15:12ff, follows a very similar format.

The author of our framework certainly means to represent what follows as a victory song. He is almost surely basing himself on 1 Sm 18:6f and probably knows Jg 11:34 as well.

Victory songs always have women among the performers; beside the above texts, see Jg 5:1. And the author of the framework represents the women as singing in the Song's performance.

The placement of the Song immediately after the prose account in Ex 14 also is indicative that the framework composers considered it a victory song. Normally such pieces come immediately after the prose account, see Jg 4 followed by 5, 11:34 after 11:32f, 16:23f after 16:21, Jdt 16 after 15.

We also find that the framework has reference to concrete participants and events. The rubrics mention Moses and Miriam, vv 1a, 20a, 21a. The resume mentions Pharaoh and the Sons of Israel, v 19ab. So also in all the other victory songs in the Old Testament, their prose frameworks contain concrete reference to participants and/or events of the previous prose account, see Jg 5:1; 11:34; 16:23; 1 Sm 18:6; Jdt 15:12ff.

It is clear that the framework composers knew the victory song form very well, and intended the Song of the Sea to be treated as one. It is also evident that they wrote the framework with the idea of inserting the Song after the prose account of the victory at the Reed Sea recounted in Ex 14.

Indications in the Song

The Song itself gives numerous indications that it is a victory song. V 1b sets the tone for all of part one. God has thrown the cavalrymen into the sea. The phrase of 2aβ, "And he has been salvation for me," is originally a statement about help received by an ally in battle, 2 Sm 10:11, cf Is 63:8. Yahweh is styled a man of war in 3a. He throws the chariots into the sea, 4a; he destroys the enemy by his right hand, 6b, 12. God is represented as fiercely angry, 7, 8aα, and the breath of that anger destroys the enemy, 10. V 9 represents a sudden shift into the mind of the enemy where he gleefully expects to share out the spoil. That same sudden shift of scene and expectation of spoil can be seen in the song of Deborah and Barak, Jg 5:28-30.

Also, part one makes specific reference to the historical event, Pharaoh and the Reed Sea, v 4. This concrete reference is a trait found in all victory songs. Jg 5 mentions Deborah, Barak, Sisera, etc. Jg 16:23f speaks of Sampson, 1 Sm 18:7 praises David and Saul, Jdt 16 talks of Judith and Assyria.

In the second part the victory song motif is not as evident, but it is still present. The Song mentions the peoples in general and then lists the Philistine, Edomites, Moabites, and the Canaanites, vv 14-16a. What is unusual here is that there is mention of enemies that will be encountered only in the future. But the defeat of God's future enemies is also found in the other instances of a developed victory song form, very briefly in Jg 5:31aα, then in a more developed way in Jdt 16:17.

Also, in the second part the people are placed in a situation of perfect safety, for they are brought into God's own dwelling where he himself reigns forever, vv 13, 17f. This motif of being established in a definitive mode appears briefly in Jg 5:31aβ, then more developed in Jdt 16:15f. In the Song, then, we have the defeat of the future enemies and the security of the friends of God in a developed form.

The conclusion is that the Song is a victory song, and that both parts one and two can fall under the umbrella of that form.

A note on the proto-apocalyptic form of the Song

It is then very important to note that the elements of the future victory of God over all his foes and the perfect security of his people are not original to the early form of the victory song. Jg 5:31a, which contains these elements, is a psalmic verse added for adaptation to the cult[7]. It has a very strong resemblance to Ps 92:10, which we have already noted is considered by most to be post-exilic. The other instance where these elements are present is the very late song of Judith, where they are developed and integrated into the form. It is very possible that these elements, especially in the developed form in which they are found in the Song, represent a post-exilic notion of what is involved in a victory song.

This, along with other characteristics noted above, place the whole of the Song of the Sea into the form of proto-apocalyptic.

---

7   C. F. Burney, *The Book of Judges*, The Library of Biblical Studies (New York: KTAV, 1970) 157; Jacob M. Myers, "The Book of Judges," *The Interpreter's Bible*, vol. 2 (Nashville: Abingdon, 1953) 728f.

The victory of God over the elements and their convulsion, v 7, and the use of myth forms, vv 5-18 passim (see pp 98f below), combined with ultimate and never ending victory over all enemies and the perfect security of his people, vv 10, 13-17, are indicators that we are on the road toward apocalyptic. Also of this genre is the representation that God alone works the victory and the salvation; the people of Israel are never mentioned at all in the first part of the Song. Also of the type is the passive representation of the people, vv 13, 17. The concluding doxology about God's future rule, which is eternal, v 18, establishes within the Song a definite eschatological vision and completes this quasi-apocalyptic picture. The degree of development of apocalyptic elements is far beyond its roots in the victory song form. That the Song is proto-apocalyptic is indicative of a genre development of the post-exilic period.

Cult Character

Indications in the framework

It is rather clear that the prose framework presents a set of instructions for the cult performance of the Song. There seem to have been two choruses, one of men, "Then sang Moses and all the Sons of Israel," v 1a, and then a dancing chorus of women, v 20. The head of the men took the part of Moses, and the head of women took the part of Miriam. These were probably soloists because the Song begins in the first person singular, v 1b, "I will sing," and continues in the first person through v 2. And in v 20f it says that all the women went out after Miriam, but it only speaks of her singing to the men, v 21a.

The first verse of the Song is used as a refrain by the women, v 1b, 21b. In being used as a refrain the form is changed from the first person intention to praise, אָשִׁירָה, to the third person invitation to praise, שִׁירוּ. The refrain was perhaps repeated at various times in the performance. Also, in the rubrics there is reference to all the Sons of Israel. Thus there is indicated a major feast when all of Israel was required to be present, Ex 23:17; Dt 16:16; Js 8:33; 24:1.

The Song itself also gives repeated indications of liturgical use in the cult. The phrase, "my strength and my song is Yah," v 2a, contains the form זִמְרָת, which can only really be explained as a cult form. First, the term in itself means my song, from the root זמר, to sing[8]. It stands for the expected זִמְרָתִי, my song. The term before it, עָזִּי, contains the first person ending, and this is connected to by the copulative "and"; so that זִמְרָתִי, זִמְרָה with the first person ending, would be expected. Also, all the surrounding material is in the first person, and where applicable, has the first person endings, אָבִי, אֵלִי, לִי. Thus the form requires an explanation. The only enduring reason that has been given is that it is a shortened form of זִמְרָתִי resulting from liturgical use, and that זִמְרָת יָהּ is a cult shout mode[9].

יָהּ, v 2aα, itself only appears as a cult form (see pp 67-69 below). Also the introductory statement of v 2b, "this is my God," is best explained as cultic confessional.

The term תְהִלֹת, v 11b, means praiseworthy deeds, those that give rise to celebration in the cult.

The acclamations, vv 6, 11, 16b, all include Yahweh in the vocative. It could be translated "Oh Yahweh." This direct address

---

8   There have been attempts to link this form to a root meaning shield, but the weight of evidence still rests on the older translation. For a resume of the discussion see G. Johannes. Botterweck and Helmer Ringgren, *Theological Dictionary of the Old Testament*, vol. 4, trans. David Green (Grand Rapids: Eerdmans, 1980) 94.

9   Hans Bauer and Pontus Leander, *Historische Grammatik der Hebräischen Sprache des Alten Testamentes* (Hildesheim: Georg Olms, 1962) 603g.

form thus represents a shout that appears three times. Such a configuration demands cult use.

All of the second part has the theme of Yahweh leading the people and therefore going at their head, and he leads them into a sacred area, v 13b. The place of arrival is described specifically as a מִקְדָּשׁ, sanctuary, in v 17b. The use of קֹדֶשׁ immediately brings up cultic connotation. And the notion of God going before the people into the sanctuary is the description of cult procession and temple entrance.

The expression "Yahweh will reign forever and ever," v 18, is beyond the flow of the action and is only explained as also being a shout. Its appearances in psalmic literature are always concerning the cult, Ps 47:9; 93:1; 96:10; 97:1; 99:1, 4; 146:10. The expression לְעֹלָם וָעֶד, forever and ever, especially in its present position at the end of the psalm, is formulaic of the cult, see Ps 48:15; 45:18; 145:21.

The overall conclusion is that the Song of the Sea was written as a cult piece and that its usages can only be explained by active cult use.

The Prose Framework, vv 1a, 19, 20, 21a

Analysis of the rubrics, vv 1a, 20, 21a

The introduction to the singing of the Song, Ex 15:1a, has an almost exact verbal correspondence to Nb 21:17. The only difference is that Moses is not mentioned. The short song that it introduces is generally held to be very ancient and perhaps from pre-Israelite times, but the introduction of this poem into the Pentateuch is considered to be in a later stage of redaction and is never identified with J, E or P[10]. The introductory verse would be part of the redactor's work, and, therefore, late and not related to the early sources.

Ex 15:1a also demonstrates similarities with the verses introducing two songs that have been added to Deuteronomic works. The Song of Moses is introduced by Dt 31:19, 21, 22, 30, see also 32:44, David's song by 2 Sm 22:1, 2a. its parallel in Ps 18:1, 2a depends on it.

The introduction of the Song of Moses is found within sections that are according to the style of the Deuteronomist, Dt 31:16-22, 28-30; 32:44. These sections are from the latest stage of Deuteronomistic redaction[11]. David's song is part of a series of additions that break the action between 2 Sm 20:26 and 1 Kg 1:1, and, therefore, after the work of the Deuteronomistic editors. Much of the material is old, but the phrase introducing this psalm must be from the editor and post-Deuteronomic.

Thus, the introductory verse is of a formulation that is nowhere identified with the J, E or P source. It is of a very general nature for use to make additions to an already formulated text. Where identifiable, the form occurs late. It was in use in Deuteronomistic and post-Deuteronomic circles. It has already been shown that vv 20, 21a have a very close resemblance to two texts within the D source material, 1 Sm 18:6f, Jg 11:34; so that wherever contact with a source is verifiable, it is within the D stream.

In v 20 we also find that Miriam is called a prophetess while she is in the act of dancing in procession and performing responsorial singing of standard psalmic formulation. The notion that women functioned as prophets occurs throughout the Old Testament, Jg 4:4; Is 8:3; 2 Kg 22:14 = 2 Chr 34:22; Neh 6:14.

---

10 Martin Noth, *Numbers: A Commentary*, trans. James D. Martin, The Old Testament Library (Philadelphia: Westminster, 1968) 159.

11 S. L. Moran, "Deuteronomy," *A New Catholic Commentary on Holy Scripture*, rev. ed. (Surrey: Nelson, 1975) 257 par g.

And there does seem to be a tradition that Miriam carried out the function of transmitting prophetic communications from God to the people, Nb 12:2, 6.

But the specific notion that this text conveys is that in the action of cult psalm singing, dancing, and playing of tambourine she is functioning as a prophet. From the most ancient times prophets functioned in procession in concert with musical instruments, 1 Sm 10:5f, 10. But the practice described does not indicate that there was singing by the prophets; the musical instruments are used to promote a trance. There are other texts, though, where the musical instruments promote a trance in which the prophet prophesies, 2 Kg 3:15ff. But again, it is not singing that is described. The prophecy that ensues has a semi-poetic quality, but cannot be called song.

The act of prophecy itself can be called the singing of a song. Isaiah prophesies against Israel, probably during the celebrations after the grape harvest, and there is poetic rhythm there, Is 5:1-7. Yet Isaiah's recital cannot be termed psalmic verse.

According to the editors of the book of Jg a prophet can perform an actual song. Deborah was a prophetess and also the singer of the victory song, Jg 5:1[12]. Still, her singing is not considered a prophecy, because Barak, who is not a prophet, sings the song with her.

Thus, there is a long tradition connecting prophecy with musical instruments and the singing of poetry. But what is described in the framework of the Song is specifically psalm performance. The picture given is one of highly structured responsorial singing between choirs of men and women. Psalm singing is described as prophecy only by the Levitical singing

12 Jg 5:1 is most likely redactional, see George F. Moore, *Judges*, The International Critical Commentary (Edinburgh: T and T Clark, 1908) 137.

choirs of the second temple, 1 Chr 25:1-3; 2 Chr 35:15. These groups seem to have considered themselves as taking over the functions of the prophets of the pre-exile, see 2 Chr 20:14f, 20.

In the text of 1 Chr 25:1-7 the three groups of temple singers are described as prophets. Within the clan of Heman his daughters are also mentioned as forming a performing choir, and they, like their brothers, are placed at the side of their father, who is styled a prophet, 25:5f.

Then Miriam is further described as the sister, אָחוֹת, of Aaron. This description has always caused a difficulty because Aaron does not perform any function in the piece. But this manner of describing Miriam also has its explanation within the mentality of the second temple Levites. They described themselves as brothers of the Aaronic priests to emphasize their common origin and to enhance their status. The claim appears within the context of the above mentioned texts: 1 Chr 23:32; 24:31; 2 Chr 35:6, 14f. Elsewhere it is found in 29:34; Ezr 3:8f; 6:20; Neh 13:13. Thus, the formula of Ex 15:20 is a description of the singers as Levites. That Miriam is called sister of Aaron indicates the notion that the function of the female singers was Levitical in nature.

If this analysis is correct, the formulation must be post-exilic, because the singers of the temple did not have Levitical status on their return from the exile. The list of the returning exiles distinguishes them from the Levites, Ezr 2:40f = Neh 7:43f. But they did lay hold of this status after the return, Ezr 3:10.

Thus, vv 1a, 20, 21a of the prose framework are not identifiable with the J, E or P sources. The form of v 1a, when it appears elsewhere, always is used by redactors to make psalmic additions. The material used in vv 1a, 20, 21a is either D influenced or appears in Deuteronomistic and post-Deuteronomic additions to D works. The fact that Miriam is called prophetess and sister of Aaron places these verses among the Levites of the second temple.

The prose explanation, v 19

An examination of the explanatory verse, Ex 15:19, will reveal the same characteristics, that it has D roots and is to be placed among the post-exilic Levites. We begin by noting that as a whole the three phrases that constitute this verse have a very close correlation to the phrasing found in the P source in Ex 14. 15:19aα can be compared with 14:9, 17, 23, 28, all P[13]. The verses are virtually the same in vocabulary, usage and phrasing.

15:19aβ has a relation to the mode of portrayal found in both the JE and the P source. The formulation וַיָּשָׁב...הַיָּם , can be compared with Ex 14:27aβ, J, וַיָּשָׁב הַיָּם. The formulation of the whole phrase has a stronger correspondence to P. Compare הַיָּם...עֲלֵהֶם...מֵי הַיָּם וַיָּשָׁב with 14:26, ...עַל הַמַּיִם וְיָשֻׁבוּ הַיָּם But in neither case can we speak of a real correspondence in the phrasing.

But in 15:19b we find an exact duplicate of 14:29a, P, and it is found virtually intact in 14:16b, 22a, also P. Also to be noted is that the conjunction of events as described in all of v 19 is the same as in 14:28, 29, a P text.

Despite this virtual duplication of P verses, these lines are not the creation of the P redactor. To begin, the P redactor is never interested in adapting song for cult use. Then, v 19 cannot be adequately described as simply quotations strung together. It has a rhythmic quality to it. The verses are each of about the same length, five or six beats, and they end with הַיָּם or בַּיָּם. It has a quality that is itself semi-poetic and is a well

---

13 Source analysis of Ex 14 follows J. Phillip Hyatt, *A Commentary on Exodus*, New Century Bible (London: Oliphants, 1971) 148. He, like most recent commentaries, follows Noth 105f, with slight divergences.

constructed artistic unity. Then, all the material of v 19aα and its P correlates appears first in D. They can be compared with Js 24:6, Dt 11:3f.

Ex 15:19aα	Dt 11:3f	Js 24:6
בָּא...בַּיָּם		תָּבֹאוּ הַיָּמָּה
סוּס	לְסוּסָיו	
לְפַרְעֹה	לְפַרְעֹה	
בְּרִכְבּוֹ וּבְפָרָשָׁיו	וּלְרִכְבּוֹ	בְּרֶכֶב וּבְפָרָשִׁים
בַּיָּם		יַם־סוּף

The phrase "and you went to the sea" in Js 24:6 is of the Israelites, not of the Egyptians, and it describes the Israelites going up to, not into, the sea. But I have included it because the phrase implicitly applies to the Egyptians who pursued the Israelites, and it is easy to see how the phrasing could later be accommodated to the passing through the waters, with the development of the crossing tradition.

The relationship of dependence between the Song, P, and D is not clear at this point, but we can still note certain things: The two D texts involved are from a very late period of redaction. Dt 11 is part of the work of the last Deuteronomistic historian[14], and so not earlier than the exile. Js 24 is from the post-Deuteronomic Levitical redactors using Deuteronomistic traditions[15], thus later than Dt 11, but with material of the same era. Many hold, though, that Js 24 is an editing of older traditions according to the late Deuteronomistic mind set, but the presence of the redactor is extremely heavy[16]. I note that the passage in

---

14 A. D. H. Mayes, *Deuteronomy*, New Century Bible (Grand Rapids: Eerdmans, 1981) 207f.

15 A. D. H. Mayes, *The Story of Israel between Settlement and Exile* (London: SCM Press, 1983) 51ff.

16 J. Maxwell Miller and Gene M. Tucker, *The Book of Joshua*, The Cambridge Biblical Commentary (Cambridge, 1974) 179.

question is thoroughly Deuteronomistic in its language. Compare for example Js 24: 5aβ, 7abβ with Dt 11:5a, 7, 4:9aβ, 12bβ.

The Deuteronomistic and post-Deuteronomic material cannot be derived from P because the latest redactors claim that it derives from the north, especially from Shechem, see Dt 11:29f, Js 24:1, and P was a southern source. The material in question is not ancient in its phrasing and can only have a remote connection to the recitations at the northern shrines, but the claim for northern origin would not be consonant with a simple takeover from P. So for the line of dependence, P rests on D.

The Song of the Sea then can be placed also after the Deuteronomistic texts and in dependence on them, because its formulations are so close to P. The examination of v 19aα cannot, though, tell us whether the Song is in the line of the D tradition development or in that of P.

More revealing, however, is the structure of v 19aβ. Here God brings the waters back on the Egyptians. The vocabulary is similar to P but the formulation and concept are specific and restricted to the D source, not P. The D recitations portray God bringing back the waters by the use of the *hiph'il*. Also, the other forms and usages in the line have an exact correspondence to D. Compare:

Ex 15:19aβ	וַיָּשֶׁב (*hiph'il*)	יהוה עַל ...... הֶם אֶת מֵי הַיָּם	
Dt 11:4	הֵצִיף (*hiph'il*)	אֶת מֵי יַם־סוּף	
		עַל פְּנֵי הֶם	
Js 24:7	וַיָּבֵא (*hiph'il*)	עָל ...... יו אֶת הַיָּם	

The correspondence is accentuated because Yahweh is also the actor in the Deuteronomistic texts. So that whoever is constructing v 19 has arrived at formulations that are identical in places with P, but in 19aβ he shows that he has the Deuteronomistic mind set. Actually, the exactitude with which our text corresponds to the P source could be explained as a literary quote, but the unmistakable congruence with the D form with variations is a compelling indicator that our author thinks like the Deuteronomistic redactor and the post-Deuteronomic developers of the D tradition.

V 19b and its P correlates can be compared with Js 4:22f, a Deuteronomistic text[17], Neh 9:11, a text of the second temple Levites with a great deal of Deuteronomistic formulation, Nb 33:8, a P text (see pp 89f below), and Ps 136, a work of the second temple Levites that shows signs of both D and P influence (see p 92).

Ex 15:19b	Js 4:22f	Neh 9:11	Nb 33:8	Ps 136:14, 13
וּבְנֵי יִשְׂרָאֵל הָלְכוּ	יִשְׂרָאֵל			יִשְׂרָאֵל
	עָבַר	וַיַּעַבְרוּ	וַיַּעַבְרוּ	הֶעֱבִיר
בַּיַּבָּשָׁה	בַּיַּבָּשָׁה	בַּיַּבָּשָׁה		
בְּתוֹךְ הַיָּם		בְּתוֹךְ־הַיָּם	בְּתוֹךְ־הַיָּם	בְּתוֹכוֹ
	יַם־סוּף			יַם־סוּף

Also here the development of the tradition that results in the formulation of Ex 15:19b has its first literary appearance in the Deuteronomistic redactors, in this case in Js 4:22. And again the formulation begins in the exile, because the way that it is formulated in the Deuteronomistic redactors gives firm indication that it begins with them.

Before the Deuteronomistic redactors there is never any mention, in any tradition, of a going into or a crossing of the Reed Sea. Before them there is a very old tradition of going into and crossing of the Jordan River, and the JE traditions about deliv-

---

17 Miller and Tucker 42.

erance at the Sea, but not one that includes entering or crossing the sea as part of that deliverance. Only with Js 4:22f do we have the explicit statement of the crossing of the Reed Sea, a crossing that the author can formulate because he has equated the River and the Sea experiences, 4:23. This equation of River and Sea is also original to the Deuteronomistic redactors and never appears earlier than this text. That the River is a redoing of the Sea allows for the formulation of the Sea event in terms that were earlier only applied to the River; what was predicated of the River must be predicable of the Sea.

We can see this taking place if we examine the use of יַבָּשָׁה for dry land. It is not part of the early tradition of either the Sea or River traditions, but first appears in the Deuteronomistic redactors treating the Jordan river crossing in this text, Js 4:22f. The word is applied by that text to describe also the Sea crossing and then enters into the later Sea traditions.

Once we concede that the formulation can be no older than the exile, we must further conclude that the text must be post-exilic and of the second temple, because it was certainly used within a cult performance which is an entrance into a physical shrine. Although some worship seems to have existed in the Exile, there is no indication that any shrines were ever used[18]; the Deuteronomic dictate that valid worship could only be performed in Jerusalem had won out within the Jewish community as a whole. Thus, entering a shrine can only be of Jerusalem and after the return.

The formulation then appears in post-exilic Levitical works, Neh 9 and Ps 136, a work of the second temple Levitical singers, (see pp 63, 182 below), as well as in the P source itself, Nb 33:8, Ex 14:29. Thus, if we leave P, who is not interested in

---

18 Roland de Vaux, *Ancient Israel its Life and Institutions*, trans. John McHugh (London: Darton, Longman and Todd, 1961) 339.

cult rubrics for psalm singing, out of consideration as composers of Ex 15:19b, we confront elements that we have seen before, a tradition that begins in the Deuteronomistic redactor and appears, in the time frame which interest us, in the works of the Levites.

Left unresolved is the relation of dependence between the prose summary and P. The problem is rendered difficult because, as is obvious already, both P and the prose framework are after the D traditions. But if we follow the common opinion of exegetes that the basic P redaction of the Pentateuch was done in Babylon, then we have to posit that Ex 15:19b was written after the equivalent P texts of Ex 14. This is because Ex 15:19 was written for active cult use, and so for the Jerusalem temple, which dictates a place of composition within the land of Judah. Also, it is part of a framework that was written for insertion after a prose text. And the framework presents it as a victory song, clearly to celebrate the victory as told in Ex 14. The text of Ex 14 to which it was added would have to be the already P redacted version. We can know this because the first time the Jerusalem cult community would have had access to a version of the Pentateuch would almost certainly have been on the return of Ezra. The version that he brought back is considered by most critics to have been one redacted by P. Therefore, the authors had the P redacted version of Ex 14 available when they wrote.

This is confirmed by the fact that Ps 106:12 knows the Song as placed after the P redacted version of Ex 14 (see pp 183f).

Thus, we can conclude that Ex 15:19 was written with Ex 14 in mind and to conform to the story portrayed there, but in such a way that it betrays its D roots.

It follows then that we must look for the authors of the prose summary among a group which is involved in the transmission of the D tradition. The classic position has been that the Levites from the shrines of the North who escaped to the South after the fall and brought with them northern traditions were the compilers and editors of the Deuteronomic and later the Deuteronomistic corpus[19]. But that position has been questioned, and attempts have been made to identify the Deuteronomists with the wise men in the court of Hezekiah[20], the prophetic circles[21], or disenfranchised Levites in the south[22]. Each of these positions has its difficulties, and the northern Levites hypothesis seems to still best fit all of the evidence.

For our purposes, though, the early disposition of the D tradition is not vital. What we need to know is what post-exilic group inherited the D tradition and specifically its Deuteronomistic development. On this question A. D. H. Mayes has demonstrated the existence of a post-Deuteronomic level in the D corpus that is easily identifiable with Levites who are interested in the cult and have a strong identification with the shrine at Shechem[23]. They are the ones intrusted with the Deuteronomic tradition and Law, at least by the time of the exile, Dt 31:25f, and they appear after the exile as explainers of the Law at the return of Ezra in Neh 8, a text that consciously presents them as fulfilling the role mapped out in Dt. 31:25f. So for composers of the Song's prose framework, which has a cultic function and which presents material from D, Deuteronomistic and post-Deuteronomic traditions, we should look to them.

---

19 For a summary of the position and the evidence see N. Lohfink, "Deuteronomy," *The Interpreter's Dictionary of the Bible*, Supplementary Volume (Nashville: Abingdon, 1976) 229f.

20 Moshe Weinfeld, *Deuteronomy and the Deuteronomic School* (Oxford: Clarendon, 1972) 158ff.

21 Ernest W. Nicholsen, *Deuteronomy and Tradition* (Oxford: Basil Blackwell, 1967) 69ff, 117f.

22 Mayes, *Deuteronomy* 103-108.

23 Mayes, *Story* 51-57.

Moreover, the closeness to the formulation of the P redactor would also bespeak the Levites, who, because of the nature of their office, were in constant contact with the priests.

Thus, all of the framework, 15:1a, 19-21a, evidences the same milieu of composition, the Levites of the second temple carrying out a post-Deuteronomic usage of Deuteronomic and Deuteronomistic traditions.

CHAPTER THREE
ANALYSIS OF THE FORMULAIC ENCLOSURE
VV 1b-3, 18, 21b

The Cult Milieu of the Enclosure

Vv 1b, 2 have a very close relationship to both Ps 118 and to post-exilic liturgical psalmic redactions in the book of the prophet Isaiah. The Isaian texts comprise Is 12:1-3, 4-6; 25:1, 9; 26:1f. The similarities that exist between the Song formulas, Ps 118, and the set of redactive texts in Isaiah are so strong that they can only be explained by a period of common cult style. I postulate that the authorship of all three sets of texts comes from one literary circle.

The unity of the Isaian texts, Is 12:1-3, 4-6; 25:1, 9; 26:1f

These texts constitute a complete set introduced for the purpose of liturgical redaction in first Isaiah. It is not necessary that they were introduced at the same moment of redaction, but they are clearly of the same school and period. The texts are generally introduced by the formula, "And you will say on that day," or something equivalent in structure and sense. See 12:1, 4; 25:9; 26:1. Only 25:1 does not have the formula, but it is clearly of the same stylistic school. It can be compared in its structure with 12:1.

כִּי (vocative) יהוה ךָ אוֹדְ		12:1
כִּי	אוֹדְה שִׁמְךָ ... (vocative) יהוה	25:1

Also, 26:1b shows the same general language usage as 12:2, except that it speaks in the first person plural instead of the singular, and it applies terms used for Yahweh in 12:2 to the city and its walls that Yahweh has built. 26:1b, יְשׁוּעָה, לָנוּ עָז, compares with 12:2, עָזִי, יְשׁוּעָתִי, לִי, לִישׁוּעָה.

Comparison of the Song and the Isaian texts

These texts as a whole show a very strong coincidence of vocabulary, phrasing, usage, and style with the introductory formulas of the Song of the Sea. The first of these is Is 12:1-3. 12:2b is the exact duplicate of v 2a of the Song, with the addition of an explanatory יהוה after יָהּ. This phrase occurs elsewhere only in Ps 118:14.

12:5aα is the counterpart to the first half of the refrain of the Song found in vv 1bα and 21bα.

The first person exaltation phrase with five consecutive words beginning with א found in v 2b of the Song corresponds to the opening psalm verse of Is 25:1a, which is a four א first person exaltation phrase. Elsewhere this type of acclamation only occurs in Ps 118:28.

The expression זֶה אֵלִי of v 2bα of the Song has the form: זֶה + a divine name. This form appears in Is 25:9b. This specific form appears elsewhere only in Psalm 48:15 and Neh 9:18, which will be discussed below.

Also, the same mentality of זֶה אֵלִי is definitely present in Is 12:2, הִנֵּה אֵל יְשׁוּעָתִי.

The placement of the Isaian texts

There is general agreement that the Isaian texts are late and of the second temple[1], and they are then, naturally, of a secondary level of redaction and placed within the text of first Isaiah. They were used to convert the book of Isaiah to the cult[2].

In addition, there is evidence for stating that this redactive enterprise extended down to the time of the completion of the walls by Nehemiah. There is mention of a processional entrance during a feast that celebrated the walls of a city, 26:1f. The city must be Jerusalem because the celebration is in Judah in the latter times, 26:1. Besides, 12:6 and 24:23b specify that Yahweh's residence in the temple on Zion is being proclaimed. Also, the walls have just been completed, because the redactor celebrates the fact that Yahweh has set up the walls. This completion is seen as a victory for Yahweh, 25:9. A psalmic piece celebrating the just completed walls, whose completion is conceived of as a victory, is best placed at the celebration of the completion of the walls by Nehemiah, which was considered a victory over the surrounding peoples, who threatened to stop the project by force of arms.

Is 26:1, 2   In that day this song will be sung in the land of Judah,

"We have a strong city.

He (Yahweh) has set up walls and ramparts for salvation.

Open the gates, and let in a righteous nation, which keeps faith."

---

1   Otto Kaiser, *Isaiah 1-12: A Commentary*, trans. R. A. Wilson, The Old Testament Library (Philadelphia: Westminster, 1972) 167; *Isaiah 13-39: A Commentary*, trans. R. A. Wilson, The Old Testament Library (Philadelphia: Westminster, 1974) 173; George Buchanan Gray, *The Book of Isaiah: I-XXVII*, The International Critical Commentary (Edinburgh: T and T Clark, 1912) 229, 403.

2   J. Lindblom, *Prophecy in Ancient Israel* (Philadelphia: Fortress, 1962) 284.

The non-derived quality of the Isaian texts

The correspondence of these texts in Isaiah to the Song verses is such that they cannot be considered a quotation or usage of the Song in a later period. I maintain this because the language that it holds in common with the Song is proper to the Isaian texts, and the style devices that it has in common with the Song are fully integrated within its own stylistic mentality. The style of the Isaian texts must be a product of its own cult milieu and originate there.

The demonstration of this begins with an examination of Is 12:2b and Ex 15:2a. It has already been shown that the form זִמְרָת is a shortened form of זִמְרָתִי and that it has its present form only because it makes the phrase apt for cult use. This ungrammatical form would be very difficult to transmit in a purely literary milieu for an extended period of time; it would eventually be emended. Therefore, this active cult form would indicate that we are in the same cult period, the post-exile.

It can then be noted that יְשׁוּעָה is proper to the Isaian redactor. It is present three times in a concentrated space, 12:2ab, 3. Its concentrated appearances continue as a part of the style of the redactor elsewhere, 25:9ab; 26:1. Moreover, we have seen that the vocabulary of Is 12:2b appears again in Is 26:1. Therefore, the usages were part of the milieu of the psalmic redactor. Is 12:2b; 25:9; 26:1b are all natural phrasing from within a style that properly belongs to this author.

We can then compare Is 12:5a to Ex 15:1b*a*

> שִׁירוּ לַיהוה כִּי גָאֹה גָּאָה   Ex 15:21b
> זַמְּרוּ יהוה כִּי גֵאוּת עָשָׂה   Is 12:5a

Is 12:5a is the closest verse in Scripture to the Song's phrase. But an examination of these two verses reveals that while you do not have a quotation, you do have real equivalence of poetic phrasing. The conjunction of the same vocabulary, equivalent wording, sound value, rhythm, and conceptual sense indicates that the same style is present in both verses. But style cannot be quoted. Style belongs to a period, and if there is an attempt to imitate style, there are usually clear indicators to the effect. But exactly the opposite signs are present in the Isaian text. The phrasing of Is 12:5a is part of his own style, and spans the work. It can be compared with 12:1a, ...כִּי יְהוָה אוֹדְךָ. It also has a clear resonance with Is 25:1, ...יְהוָה...אוֹדְךָ...כִּי עָשִׂיתָ.

Similarly when we look at the alliteration phrases, Is 25:1a, Ex 15:2b, it is immediately apparent that the two texts are of the same style. The phenomenon of א repeated more than three times appears five times in the scriptures: twice in the Song of the Sea, here, in Ps 118:28, and in Is 46:4. And the exaltation vocabulary within the phrase restricts it to Ex 15:2b, here, and Ps 118. But again, it is just as apparent that the Isaiah text is acting according to its own parameters. As a whole they are thanksgiving texts, hence the use of "I will thank" instead of "I will adorn with praise." And we have already shown that Is 25:1a is of the same poetic mind as 12:1a, because of the presence of the respective sequences: ...כִּי ךָ...אוֹדְךָ, and אוֹדְךָ יְהוָה כִּי . The author is moving freely, using what is surely his own phrasing according to the liturgical form of the piece.

The form זֶה + the deity, Is 25:9ba, cannot be present by chance, and therefore is related to v 2ba of the Song. But again, the form pertains to the Isaian redactor. Its equivalent appears within the same verse, 25:9a, "This is the one we have waited for." Furthermore, it is an integral part of an acclamation where it completes and clarifies the first זֶה phrase, that is, it explains who is the one they have waited for. It flows within the verse as necessary. Also, it can be noted that the form is very similar to the acclamation style we have seen in vv 6, 11, 16b of the Song. Here the sequencing is a/b/c; a/Yahweh/d. Hence, there is a very strong concentration of stylistic elements present, all of which demonstrate the same stylistic mind and none of which can be copied. Styling can have a long life, but the intensity of overall agreement of style found consistently in these two works is too great to be explained by a chance occurrence separated by centuries.

Moreover, the other equivalent to the זֶה phrase, Is 12:2a*a*, has the same meaning and poetic movement that is found in the Song phrase. In addition, it is within context, so to speak:

Ex 15:2ab*a* עָזִּי וְזִמְרָת יָהּ   וַיְהִי לִי לִישׁוּעָה זֶה אֵל   יְ

Is 12:2 ...י הִנֵּה אֵל יְשׁוּעָתִ

עָזִּי וְזִמְרָת יָהּ יהוה וַיְהִי לִי לִישׁוּעָה

It is very clear that we are within the same mentality, but it is equally clear that simple dependence of one text on the other does not explain the evidence.

Moreover, the above investigation reveals other poetic technique that is present in both sets of texts. אוֹדְךָ in Is 12:1 appears in 25:1 as אוֹדֶה שִׁמְךָ. The original word and its ending appear with an intervening word between them, in this case שֵׁם, but the same meaning is portrayed in both instances. That can be compared with בְּרוּחֲךָ, Ex 15:10a, and בְרוּחַ אַפֶּיךָ, 15:8a, with רוּחַ as the intervening word. Then the sound technique can be seen within the Song's formulaic introduction itself in אֵלִי and אֱלֹהֵי אָבִי, 15:2b.

When all of the Isaian redactive texts are taken into account, it is noted that the whole of the formulaic liturgical language that is present in vv 1b, 2, 21b of the Song is present there also. The basic difference between the two texts is that the Song of the Sea is a victory Song and the Isaian texts have a thanksgiving format. Therefore, the phrase "Horse and rider he has cast into the sea" has no correlative in the Isaian texts, because that is what specifies our text to the victory song form and the circumstance of the deliverance at the Sea. But despite the differences of liturgical form, the general liturgical language that is revealed underneath both works is so close that the same period, school of style and even composition within the same cultic and literary circle can be maintained.

Beside the relationship to vv 1b, 2, 21b there is also a tie between the work of the Isaian psalmic redactor and the mentality of the whole of the introductory and closing formulas within the Song, vv 1b-3, 18, 21b. If we take Is 25:1 within its redactive context of celebrating Yahweh's rule in Jerusalem, 24:23b, the following reveals itself: Yahweh, whose name is celebrated in 25:1a, is also Yahweh Sabaoth, the God of armies, the warrior, 24:23. The proclamation of the name of Yahweh who is the warrior is found in v 3 of the Song. The situation that is described in Is 24:31 is Yahweh ruling on mount Zion, surrounded by his elders. Verse 18 of the Song describes Yahweh as ruling on his mountain, v 17, among his people whom he has brought in and placed there permanently, vv 13, 16b, 17.

Conclusions regarding the enclosing formulas of the Song

The Isaian texts are all insertions into the text of Isaiah of material written by psalm composers of the second temple for adaptation to cult use. The same form is present in the enclosing formulas that set the liturgical form of the Song of the Sea. Therefore, it can be postulated that the Song section itself, vv 1b-18, 21b, was written as a piece destined for insertion after Ex 14 as part of the adaptation of the exodus prose account for cult use. So its composition post-dates the P redaction of Ex 14 and the return of Ezra. If that is granted, then it follows that both the Song and its prose framework, vv 1a, 19-21a, would have been composed in one coordinated effort for insertion within the Pentateuch in its present position.

The psalmic texts within Isaiah were placed there by people who considered that this material could be attributed to the prophet whose work they were adapting. Thus, in some way they considered themselves successors to the prophets, and the composition of psalm verse to be prophecy. This, then, is the same mentality we find within v 20 of the song, which calls Miriam the psalm verse singer a prophet.

From the evidence garnered so far, we can make a first postulation that vv 1b-3, 18, 21b of the Song of the Sea are to be placed within the circle of the psalm composers of the second temple, who also did some redactional work in the prophetic books. Then, because these verses are inseparable from the rest of the Song in time and place of composition, it can be concluded that the whole of the Song comes from this ambit.

Then, the psalm verses in Is formed part of a work that describes the entrance of the people into the city of Jerusalem in a procession that celebrated the walls that God had built. The Song too celebrates the procession of the people into the holy place that God has built, vv 13-17. If we are in the same cultic period, and everything indicates that we are, then the liturgical enclosure in the Song has the property of signaling the form of a cult procession. The completion of the building by Yahweh depicted in v 17 of the Song would indicate sometime after the successful project of Nehemiah.

Comparison of the Song with Ps 118

The other locus for the language of vv 1b, 2 is Ps 118. Ps 118:14 is the exact duplicate of v 2a, and the alliterative phrase

in v 2b is found in the same five **א** format in Ps 118:28, with a
closer concurrence of vocabulary and sequencing than we found
in the Isaiah text:

וְאַנְוֵהוּ אֱלֹהֵי אָבִי וַאֲרֹמְמֶנְהוּ   אֵלִי   Ex 15:2b

אֵלִי אַתָּה וְאוֹדֶךָ אֱלֹהַ _ יְ אֲרֹמְמֶךָּ   Ps 118:28

The texts are of the same liturgical mentality, the only difference being that God is directly addressed in Ps 118:28 and that
the phrase has a thanksgiving format.

There is no specific correspondence to vv 1b*a*, 21b*a* of the
Song, but there does exist a general correspondence of liturgical
structure. The first line of Ps 118 appears also as the last line,
and it is used as a repeated invitation to give thanks within the
psalm, vv 1, 2b, 3b, 4b, 29. That corresponds to the Song,
where the first line appears again at the end, and the line was
used in an invitation to praise form as a responsorial refrain.
The refrain in Ps 118, הוֹדוּ לַיהוָה כִּי has the same general form
as the refrain in the Song, שִׁירוּ לַיהוָה כִּי. The difference in
introductory formulas is explained by the fact that Ps 118 is a
thanksgiving piece, a הוֹדוּ work, while the Song is a victory
song and thus it has the invitation to sing. Recitation of the
first line as a repeated refrain was probably common in Israel
(see Ps 136); still, this is the only psalm in which this refrain
format is found written out fully.

The dating of Ps 118

Most modern critics place Ps 118 in the post-exile, and not a
few at the feast of Tabernacles celebrated in the time of Nehemiah
after the completion of the walls of Jerusalem[3].

---

3 Still the most complete summary of the evidence is to be found in
   Kirkpatrick 693f. See also *The New Jerusalem Bible* (Garden City:

The reasons for considering it such are cogent: The refrain of 118:1, "Give thanks to the Lord for he is good, for his love endures for ever," is characteristic of the chant of the Levite singers of the second temple. It is always in post-exilic texts that represent the situation of the second temple, and is always ascribed to the Levite singers, cf 1 Chr 16:34, 41; 2 Chr 5:13; 7:3, 6; 20:21; Ezr 3:11; Jer 33:11. It then is found only in post-exilic psalms, Ps 106:1; 107:1, 8, 15, 21, 31; 136:1 and passim[4].

Ps 118 has very strong ties to the memoirs of Nehemiah. The repetition of the words אָנָּא נָּא, v 25, is indicative of the speech patterns found in Nehemiah's personal prayer, cf Neh 1:5, 6, 8, 11. The phrase הַצְלִיחָה נָּא is the exact duplicate of Nehemiah's prayer in Neh 1:11, and this is the only time Scripture where these two roots appear together. Note that the whole pattern of Ps 118:25, אָנָּא נָּא ... הַצְלִיחָה נָּא, is present in Neh 1:1. Note also that the prayer in Neh 1:11 is for the successful rebuilding of the walls, and further on he will encourage the builders with his own confidence that God will grant success, יַצְלִיחַ, to the builders of the walls, Neh 2:20. That coordinates with the fact that the success prayer appears in Ps 118 as celebrating God's realization of the building venture, vv 22-24.

The prayer for the successful completion found in Neh 1:11 considers that it rests within the power of God, and specifically the power he showed in the exodus. This is evident from the exodus formula used in Neh 1:10. Such is the point of view evinced in Ps 118:22, because the building project carried out

---

Doubleday, 1985) note a to Ps 118.

4   The post-exilic nature of these psalms has been demonstrated by the critics. For Ps 106 see Ravasi 3:168; Kirkpatrick 624; also my discussion pp 122-124, 184f below. Ps 107 is treated in Ravasi 3:197; Kirkpatrick 637f; The New Jerusalem Bible note a to Ps 107. For Ps 136 see Ravasi 3:731; Kirkpatrick 776.

is described as נִפְלָאת, wonderful, which is the standard word for the description of the power of God displayed in the exodus event, see Ex 3:20; Jg 6:13; Ps 78:11, 32, and in the same time period as the that of Nehemiah, see Neh 9:17, Ps 106:7, 22. Also, this building entails gates, vv 19f, as did the Nehemiah's building venture, Neh 3 passim.

The attitude of not fearing man because God is with them, found in Ps 118:6, is the counterpart of how Nehemiah regards the surrounding nations who seek to stop the project, Neh 4:8, 14b. The nations that surrounded the singer of 118:10-12 can be compared to Israel's neighboring nations in Neh 4:1, and victory over them is the rebuilding of the walls, Neh 6:16. The stone that the builders rejected can be considered in the light of disparaging remarks about the building project made by Sanballat and Tobiah, the enemy leaders, see Neh 3:34-37.

The completion of the work in 118:22-24a corresponds to the same completion in Neh 6:15f. An important piece of evidence for linking Psalm 118 with this event is the close relation between vv 23, 24a with Neh 6:16. Both verses are the climax to the building endeavors, both signal the defeat of the machinations of the enemies of the building, and both place the successful completion into the person of God; it is his work. Furthermore, there is a similarity of phrasing here that is remarkable. Compare:

Ps 118:23, 24a	Neh 6:16
מֵאֵת יהוה הָיְתָה	מֵאֵת אֱלֹהֵינוּ נֶעֶשְׂתָה
זֹאת	הַמְּלָאכָה הַזֹּאת
זֶה־הַיּוֹם עָשָׂה יהוה	
בְּעֵינֵינוּ	בְּעֵינֵיהֶם

This convergence of phrasing, concept, and function in their respective texts cannot be coincidental.

And in both works there follows the celebration of the feast of Tabernacles at the temple, Ps 118:24-27, Neh 8. Compare the description of this feast as a day in which the assembly is exhorted to rejoice, 118:24, with the Levitical instructions of Neh 8:9-12. The feast of Ps 118 has its attendant procession using palm branches, vv 24-27, which corresponds to the Tabernacle celebration of Neh 8:13-18.

The many correspondences to the efforts to rebuild in Neh, and the depiction of the success of that effort in Ps 118 place it at a Tabernacle celebration after the walls were finished. It is likely that Ps 118 was written for the Tabernacle celebrated immediately after their completion.

Supportive of this conclusion is the very close relationship that Ps 118 has to the above treated redactive texts in Isaiah. Further examination will show that all of this network of psalmic verses has the strongest connection with Ps 118. The correspondence between v 14 and Is 12:2 is exact except for the added יהוה. The connection is intensified because both of these texts have the anomalous form זִמְרָת discussed above.

Again, the natural usage within each work would indicate the same cult period. We have seen the recurrence of the vocabulary of Is 12:2b in Is 26:1. See also Ps 118:21 where the last half of the phrase in v 14 is repeated.

Then, the alliterative texts of Ps 118:28 and Is 25:1 are more closely related to one another than they are to v 2b of the Song.

Ps 118:28	Is 25:1
אֵלִי	
אַתָּה	אַתָּה
אוֹדֶךָּ	אוֹדְה שִׁמְךָ
אֱלֹהַי	אֱלֹהַי
אֲרוֹמְמֶךָּ	אֲרוֹמִמְךָ

These two texts are virtually identical thanksgiving acclamations, with only some slight difference of order.

Examination of the overall thanksgiving elements in the two works reveals that both fall into the same cult period. Compare the הוֹדוּ phrases throughout:

Ps 118:19, 21, 28, 1, 29	Is 25:1; 12:2a, 4
אוֹדֶה יָהּ	אוֹדֶה שִׁמְךָ
אוֹדְךָ כִּי	אוֹדְךָ יהוה כִּי
אוֹדֶךָ	
הוֹדוּ לַיהוה כִּי	הוֹדוּ לַיהוה...כִּי

It is immediately evident that the two pieces are of the same style, which is integral to each piece. The fact that each piece is a הוֹדוּ liturgical form can only partly explain the intensity of the language agreement.

Compare also the feast acclamations of Is 25:9b and Ps 118:24. The differences in vocabulary simply underline the fact that there is an exactitude of form of liturgical usage between the two texts.

Is 25:9b	זֶה	יהוה... נָגִילָה וְנִשְׂמְחָה בִּישׁוּעָתוֹ		
Ps 118:24	זֶה ...	יהוה	נָגִילָה וְנִשְׂמְחָה ב	וֹ

The same can be said for the entrance verses in the respective works. Verses 19 and 20 of Ps 118 can both be compared with Is 26:2

Ps 118:19	Ps 118:20	Is 26:2
פִּתְחוּ־לִי שַׁעֲרֵי	זֶה־הַשַּׁעַר לַיהוה	פִּתְחוּ שְׁעָרִים
צֶדֶק אָבֹא בָם	צַדִּיקִים יָבֹאוּ בוֹ	יָבֹא גוֹי־צַדִּיק

The wording of the overall points of contact between Ps 118 and the related Isaian texts is close enough to demonstrate common circumstances, or even the same literary circles. Both Ps 118 and the Isaian texts are processional entrances into the city and the temple, both were composed within the same period, and both give every indication that they come from the time of the completion of Nehemiah's project.

The placement of the Song of the Sea in relation to Ps 118

When we examine the phrase עָזִי וְזִמְרָת יָהּ, Ps 118:14a = Ex 15:2a*a*, we note first the presence again of זִמְרָת, indicative of active cult use. We then further note that the device of ending a phrase with יָהּ is proper to the style of Ps 118, appearing in vv 5ab, 17b, 18a, 19b. It is used to give an acclamatory tone to its respective phrases, which fits the overall intensely acclamatory style of the piece. Also, it appears as part of the intensely repetitive style that pervades the work; see vv 5ab, 17b, 18a. It must be integral to the stylistic mind of the author.

Furthermore, the form יָהּ is a term of late use. It appears 22 times in the scriptures, all of them late, probably post-exilic. It is always psalmic and for cult use. It appears three times in Isaiah, Is 12:2; 26:4; 38:11. Is 26:4 is not part of a psalm; it is a piece of apocalyptic sounding poetry, but the בְּיָהּ stands completely outside the flow of the piece and is self evidently an addition and thus presumably psalmic, since the other instances of יָהּ in Is are from psalmic redactors. The other appearances, besides the five already mentioned in Ps 118, are all in higher numbered psalms: Ps 68:5, 19; 77:12; 89:9; 94:7, 12; 102:19; 115:17, 18; 122:4; 130:3; 135:4; 150:6[5].

---

5 There is general agreement in regard to all of the psalms except Ps 68. Ps 77 is always considered late; see Ravasi 2:599. *The New Jerusalem Bible* considers it post-exilic, note a to Ps 77. That dating is preferable; see my treatment pp 119f below. For Ps 89 also see my treatment pp 116-119 below. There is basic agreement on the rest: Ps 94, Ravasi 2:958f; Kirkpatrick 566; Ps 102, Ravasi 3:33-35; Kirkpatrick 592f; *The*

Of those mentioned, only Ps 68 would evokes serious disagreement among critics as to a late dating. The psalm is normally
seen to have reached its present form after a development of
earlier material for cult use. Critics disagree as to whether the
base material is ancient or late, but most hold that there was a
final cult adaptation for use of this material in the second
temple[6]. The בְּיָהּ שְׁמוֹ in v 5, and the יְהּ in v 19 are both
certainly additions because they totally break with the rhythm
and sense of what are otherwise straightforward sentences,
identifiable in both meaning and poetic form. Thus, they are
best seen as part of the final layer, so of the second temple.

יְהּ also appears in Ex 17:16, considered an E text. But the
phrase כֵּס יָהּ is corrupt and unintelligible; it is not maintained
by any of the versions, and is rejected by all the commentators[7].
This having been said, it can be affirmed all of the 21 appearances
outside of the Song are late.

Also the cult shout הַלְלוּיָהּ can be included because it is
just the one word form of הַלְלוּ יָהּ, see Ps 102:19, 115:17,
150:6. הַלְלוּיָהּ appears 24 times, all in higher numbered psalms,
all of which are usually held to be of the second temple: Ps
104:35; 105:45; 106:1, 48; 111:1; 112:1; 113:1, 9; 115:18;
116:19; 117:2; 135:1, 3, 21; 146:1, 10; 147:1, 20; 148:1, 14;
149:1, 9; 150:1, 6[8]. Of these, disagreement only occurs regard-

---

New Jerusalem Bible note a to Ps 102; Ps 115, Ravasi 3:368; Kirkpatrick
682; The New Jerusalem Bible note a to Ps 115; Ps 122, Ravasi 3:537;
Kirkpatrick 739; Ps 130, Ravasi 3:634; Kirkpatrick 758; Ps 135, Ravasi
3:710; Kirkpatrick 773; Ps 150, Ravasi 3:931; Kirkpatrick 818.

6   A summary of the opinions is found in Ravasi 2:366f, 372.

7   Childs, Exodus 311f.

8   The post-exilic provenience of the psalms in question has been
    demonstrated by the commentators: for Ps 105 see Ravasi 3:138;
    Kirkpatrick 614f; Svend Holm-Nielson, "The Exodus Tradition in Ps 105,"
    Annual of the Swedish Theological Institute 11 (1977-78): 22-30. For Ps
    111, 112, Ravasi 3:305; Kirkpatrick 671; Ps 113, Ravasi 3:337f;
    Kirkpatrick 677; Ps 116, Ravasi 3:386; Kirkpatrick 687f; Ps 117, Ravasi
    3:402; Kirkpatrick 692; Ps 146-150, Ravasi 3:931; Kirkpatrick 818.

ing the late dating of Ps 104. But most follow the Greek in placing the alleluia at the beginning of Ps 105, which is certainly of the second temple[9]. Even if the alleluia was attached to Ps 104 originally, it stands outside of the structure of the psalm and could be presumed to be an addition. So that יָהּ appears a total of 45 times outside the Song in the Old Testament and is limited to late usage. The phrase in question, Ps 118:14a, therefore, is of a form that is at home and part of the style of the psalm and uses a style that only appears in the second temple. It cannot be quoting a pre-exilic work. The phrase that 118:14a and Ex 15:2aα hold in common must be of second temple provenience.

Consideration of the second half of the line, וַיְהִי־לִי לִישׁוּעָה, reveals that לִי is part of the overall style of Ps 118; see vv 6a, 6b, 7a, 19, 21. Moreover the notion that it is God who is for the singer is the sense of vv 6a, 21b. And in vv 5b, 6a we have the conjunction of elements of the cult shout יָהּ and the following statement that Yahweh is for the singer. Compare יָהּ, יְהוָה לִי, vv 5b, 6a, with וַיְהִי לִי ... יָהּ, v 14. And each of the elements in 5b, 6a is fully integrated and flows from the repetitive style that surrounds it. The יָהּ in v 5b is the second of a series of acclamations using יָהּ. The יְהוָה לִי in 6a is followed by לִי in 6b and יְהוָה לִי in 7a. Also, v 14b appears again whole in v 21, but in the second person because it is within a phrase where God is addressed. It is eminently clear that this phrase has been generated from within the poetic style of this psalm. It is therefore demonstrable that all of the phrase in Ps 118:14 has its origin in the second temple and that the same phrase in Ex 15:2a also must have its origin from the same circumstances.

Moreover, v 14 fits very smoothly within its surrounding verses. The techniques of consonance and assonance are used

9   *The New Jerusalem Bible* note e to Ps 104.

here. There is a tight rhyme involved in the linking between עָזְרֵנִי, v 13b, and the word following, עָזִּי. Again, this word sequencing follows from within the interior thought patterns of the psalm. Compare the sequencing יְהוֹה לִי בְּעֹזְרָי, v 7a, and יְהוֹה עָזְרֵנִי ... וַיְהִי לִי, 13b, 14a. There is also a sound rhyme that following; compare לִישׁוּעָה with וִישׁוּעָה in v 15a.

Beginning the treatment of the alliteration phrase, Ps 118:28 = Ex 15:2b, we note that the thanksgiving language has already been shown to be integral to the psalm. Then, the exaltation of Yahweh, רוּם, has appeared already in v 16, יְהוֹה רוֹמֵמָה ....

Also, the use of prolonged repetition of the first vowel has appeared in v 26. Initial בּ is repeated five times, only יְהוֹה breaks the sequencing, but it appears as the second part of a word pair in the construct.

The technique of multiple alliteration extending beyond two or three words is itself a late phenomenon, appearing outside the Song in Ps 83:12; 118:26, 28; Is 46:4; 25:1; 24:2, 16. All are post-exilic, except for Is 46:4, which is exilic.

The exact cult form of זֶה + the deity, Ex 15:2bα, does not appear in Ps 118. Still, very similar forms appear in vv 20a, "This is Yahweh's gate," and 24a, "This is the day Yahweh has made." Both have the general form, זֶה ... יְהוֹה, but they refer to something that pertains to Yahweh rather than to Yahweh himself. Still, we can maintain that these forms are of the same liturgical type represented in the Song's phrase. This is apparent because the phrase of v 24a has been shown to be of exactly the same liturgical mentality and school as Is 26:9b, and in that latter phrase the formula זֶה + the deity does occur. So that the formula found in the Song has two appearances in Ps 118, and neither of these can be quotations.

If we examine this form in the scriptures as a whole, we find that besides the passages already treated, Is 25:9ab; Ps 118:20,

24, it appears elsewhere in Ps 48:15 and Neh 9:18, where it has the form of זֶה + the deity, and in Is 63:1b, where זֶה precedes a description of the deity.

Ps 48 is also a processional celebration of the walls of Jerusalem, vv 13, 14, and the walls are so closely connected with the actions of God that they are simply identified with him, v 15a. It will be demonstrated below that this psalm should also be placed at the time of the completion of Nehemiah's rebuilding project (see pp 170-174).

Neh 9:18 is certainly not a cult shout honoring Yahweh, such as we find in the other texts in question; it is a negative text recalling the molten calf incident of Ex 32:4. But it can be noted that although the Levite composers of Neh 9 are quoting in a pejorative way to demonstrate idolatry, they replace the plural and more damning אֱלֹהֶי with the singular זֶה. This would indicate a spontaneous use of a cult form current in their own day. It can also be noted that as they tell the story, they use this form to narrate a processional celebrating the bringing up of the Israelites from Egypt, see also 1 Kg 12:28. Therefore, the use here also indicates a form employed in processional liturgies sometime after the return of Ezra, thus in the general period of Nehemiah.

When we examine Is 63:1, we must take into account that the apocalypses at the end of Isaiah are fairly resistant to analysis. Most hold for some theory of development into their present form. But if we take 63:1 within its present position, we can note major similarities to the psalmic redactional texts in first Isaiah, especially those in the apocalypse of Isaiah. Is 63:1 comes as the first statement about God's utter destruction of Edom, 63:1-6. Is 25:9 introduces God's destruction of Moab, 25:10-12. In accord with the apocalyptic mentality of each text, they are speaking about ancient enemies of Israel, but these peoples can also be seen to represent the surrounding nations that opposed the rebuilding of the walls. This is supported by the fact that each composition is concerned about the rebuilding of the city's walls, a rebuilding either done or to be done by God himself, Is 26:1; 62:6, 7. Each is concerned about cult entrance, בוא, through the gates of the city, Is 26:2, 62:10, 11; 63:1. Therefore, it is possible to postulate that Is 63:1 comes from the time when there was the desire to rebuild the walls, and the time of opposition of the surrounding peoples[10]. It is also clearly for processional entrance into the city and the temple.

Thus, it is very interesting to note that this liturgical form only appears within the time of the movement to rebuild the walls. Except for Neh 9:18, which is simply quoting another text, the passages all have the mentality of God himself carrying out the building. And it is always used to represent a processional.

Also, the antiphonal structure held in common by the Song and Ps 118, the repetition of the first verse at the end and its use as a refrain, appears in Ps 118 as a product of its own cult milieu. The practice of using the particular thanksgiving line found in Ps 118:1 as an often repeated responsorial stems from within the practices of the Levitical clans of the post-exile, who use it as a refrain, I Chr 16:41; 2 Chr 5:13; 7:3, 6; 20:21; Ezr 3:11, and to begin and end their psalms with repeated use at intervals, Ps 136. See also Ps 107:1, 8, 15, 21, 31.

So it can be concluded that the points of contact between the Song of the Sea and Ps 118 really indicate the same style. There is no indication that Ps 118 depended on the Song in any of the points of contact; in fact, all points to the fact that every

---

10 John D. W. Watts, *Isaiah 34-66*, Word Biblical Commentary 25 (Waco: Word Books, 1987) 293ff, also arrives at the time of the decision of Artaxerxes to allow the rebuilding of the walls and posits 458 B. C.

bit of the phrasing and style that they hold in common has its origin from within the cult of the post-exile, particularly that cult as it flourished around the time of Nehemiah.

The elements proper to the Song

Verse 2b of the Song differs from its correlates in Is and Ps 118 in its vocabulary, which can be attributed to its form; it is a victory Song, not a thanksgiving. Therefore the verb אַנְוֵהוּ, I will adorn (with praise), is found instead of a הוֹדוּ term. It is compatible with the praise that is given in the song form. This verb traces to the root נוה and is a hapax in the Masoretic Text, but it is found elsewhere, always in late works, Sir 13:3 and post biblical Hebrew[11].

Also, the Song is celebrating a very ancient event that forms the basis of Israelite life, the exodus. Therefore, the expression "God of my father" appears instead of the simple "my God." It brings out the continuous line from the past to the present and emphasizes that the worshippers are of one piece with those who experienced the deliverance at the Sea and those who have celebrated it throughout the life of Israel. The phrase establishes the identity of the community and its roots.

The phrase "God of my father" is used in thirteen ancient texts dealing with the patriarchs. It also appears six times in the J and E exodus accounts, where Yahweh identifies himself to Moses as the God of the patriarchs. The phrase is used then sixteen times in the corpus of the Deuteronomist. Finally, it is a preferred expression in the Chronicler, occurring 33 times.

God of the father(s) is a hapax in psalmic literature, but it's appearances in other types of texts evidences that it was used in Israelite cult from early times. It appears in the cults of Beer

---

11 Foresti 43.

Sheba, Gn 26:24; 46:1, Gilead, 31:53, and Bethel, 28:13. It is a part of the foundation story of the holy place at Sinai, Ex 3:6, 13-16; 4:5.

But its appearance in the work of the Deuteronomistic redactor, Dt 26:7[12], presents this phrase within a cult context that is much closer to that of the Song. It is presented as part of a confession recalling both exodus and entrance into the land and is recited upon entrance into the shrine at Jerusalem, though by the individual worshipper, 26:2.

The phrase appears in the Song of the Sea as part of formulaic expressions that were used for intonation by the cult leader. Appearances of this phrase within that context are limited to the Chronicler. In 2 Chr 20:6 it introduces Jehosaphat's confession of faith recited in the courtyard of the temple and recalling the entrance into Canaan and the building of the temple, 20:7f. In 1 Chr 29:10, 18, 20, David is the cult leader reciting an encouragement to build the temple. Ezra intones a blessing upon reception of the rescript giving permission to rebuild the temple, Ezr 7:27.

All of the above texts have reference to the building of the temple, and all are of a liturgical form current in the second temple. 2 Chr 20:6 can be compared to Neh 9:6 regarding the subject matter. 2 Chr 20:6, 7 can be compared to Neh 9:6, 7 in regard to the use of the phrase הוּא אַתָּה, "You are he who," and the repeated use of אַתָּה in direct address praise to God. 1 Chr 29:10 is of the exact intonational form found in Neh 9:5. See also Ps 106:48, a psalm from the time after Nehemiah's success (see pp 122-124 below).

---

12 Despite the thesis of von Rad, modern commentators on Deuteronomy have reached a fairly uniform agreement that 26:5-9 is Deuteronomistic in language, see Mayes, *Deuteronomy* 334f; Weinfeld 33f.

Thus, as we get closer to the liturgical form found in the song, we see a pattern that has appeared before: a first, more general use in the Deuteronomistic redactors, then more specific usage concentrating around the liturgical practice of the second temple.

The conclusion regarding the parts of the formulas that are particular to the Song is that there is nothing about them that would weigh against their use in the post-exile around the time of Nehemiah, and the use of the phrase "God of my father," in the context in which it is found in the Song, would actually favor at least that general period.

The Doxology, v 3

In v 3 Yahweh is described as a warrior. The notion that God acted as a warrior in the exodus event is common from the beginning of Israelite history, see Ex 14:13f. But it remains to examine the form under which this concept appears in the Song.

Relation to Ps 24:7-10

There is a general resemblance to the form and meaning of this line found in Ps 24:8aβb. It has the repetition of יהוה initiating acclamatory phrases and the phrase יהוה גִּבּוֹר מִלְחָמָה is similar in form and meaning to יהוה אִישׁ מִלְחָמָה.

Then there is a general resemblance between Ps 24:7-10 as a whole and the liturgical formulaic language that begins and ends the Song. The question מִי זֶה, regarding God approaching in procession, expects an answer of the form זֶה + the name of the deity or a description of the deity, such as that found in v

2b*a* of the Song. Also, the one who is entering the sanctuary is
called king. The Song represents an entrance by Yahweh into
the sanctuary and his reign as king there is acclaimed, vv 13,
17f.

Investigation of Ps 24

Although the resemblances between Ps 24:7-10 and the Song
are too general to make an assertion that they come from the
same time period, it will still be of profit to seek to establish
above all its liturgical type and relation to other texts of interest
to us. The general opinion regarding these verses is that they
are an addition to vv 1-6, but there is widespread disagreement
in regard to the dating of the addition[13]. There are a great
number of exegetes who maintain that vv 7-10 are pre-exilic,
often noting that they bear a resemblance to the point of view
found in Is 6:1-5. In Ps 24 Yahweh is one who is at once king
and Lord of the armies, v 10; see also 7, 8, 9. In the text of
Isaiah Yahweh is also king who is Lord of armies, 6:5; see also
v 3. The gates must lift up to accommodate Yahweh in Ps 24:7,
and in Isaiah Yahweh is described as one who is high and lifted
up, Is 6:1.

Perhaps the thinking of Isaiah 6:10-5 has had an influence
on these verses, but it is impossible to make a conclusive case.
The proponents of a second temple dating note that the school
of Isaiah continued to think of God as a warrior into the later
period, and they then point out that the formulation of v 8a*βb*
has a very close resemblance to Is 42:13[14].

Virtually all of the distinctive elements in Ps 24:7-10 appear
also in the psalmic redactions of the Apocalypse of Isaiah taken

---

13 Ravasi 1:451-454.
14 Ravasi 1:453f.

within their context. The following can be compared: the gates, שְׁעָרִים, the opening, פִּתְחֵי, through which God comes, בוֹא, vv 7, 9, with the description of Is 26:2. Compare the king of glory, מֶלֶךְ הַכָּבוֹד, who is also Yahweh of hosts, יהוה צְבָאוֹת, Ps 24:7b, 10ab, with Yahweh of hosts who rules as king in his glory, Is 24:23. The question מִי זֶה, whose answer is Yahweh the warrior, of Ps 24:8ab, 10ab, finds its mate in Is 26:5, "this is Yahweh and we rejoice in his victory."

We see a similar dense correlation of elements in Ps 118. פֶּתַח, שַׁעַר, and בּוֹא describe the entrance in vv 19f. That they are found in conjunction with a זֶה acclamation, v 20, can be noted. Mention is made of the stone which is the head of the gate, רֹאשׁ, v 22, which is followed by another זֶה acclamation, v 24. That can be compared with heads of the gates in Ps 24:7, 9, followed by the זֶה question in vv 8 and 10 respectively.

Further comparison can be made with Is 63:1. The question מִי זֶה appears. The answer given is a description of Yahweh the warrior returning from a victory, 63:1b-6. In this context there is also mention of God's coming, בוֹא, 63:1; 62:11, and the gates, 62:10.

The above analysis cannot be offered as sufficient proof that Ps 24:7-10 comes from the liturgical period of the fifth century. The notion of having the gates opened so that they can be entered certainly occurs in every period. The question of dating in regard to this psalm does not seem resolvable at this time, but such a resolution is not necessary for our purposes, for the points of contact between the Song and Ps 24 are not specific enough to demand that they fall into the same time period. They are of a general cult nature that could appear over a rather long time span.

What is of use to us is that the density of the points of contact with the apocalypses of Isaiah does point out that in Ps

24 we are involved in processional with God perceived as being at the head of those entering the temple, and thus the theory that in the Song of the Sea we are confronted by a cult procession of entrance into the temple is strengthened.

Relation of v 3 to late redactional texts in the prophets

The relation of form and phrasing between v 3 of the Song and Ps 24 is not specific. When the specific forms and phrasing are found they are limited to late passages in the prophets.

The application of the phrase , man of war, to Yahweh appears only in Is 42:13.

The specific form of v 3 of the Song is only found in late doxological insertions to the prophets added for cult adaptation. The exact form of Ex 15:3 is the following: יהוה ... יהוה שְׁמוֹ. The instances in Scripture that have the phrasing יהוה שְׁמוֹ are Am 5:8; 9:6; Jer 33:2. The only other instance of a similar form appears in Ps 68:5, יָהּ שְׁמוֹ, the already mentioned cultic insertion added in the second temple.

The only instance of the whole configuration of the form found in one piece is in Jer 33:2: יהוה יֹצֵר אוֹתָהּ לַהֲכִינָהּ יהוה שְׁמוֹ. A similar configuration in form is found in the initiating and concluding phrases of Am 9:5f, which are meant to be taken together: יהוה אֱלֹהֵי הַצְּבָאוֹת ... יהוה שְׁמוֹ. The meaning is identical to the Song because lord of hosts and man of war are equivalent, Yahweh the leading warrior.

We are also in the same ambit in the doxological acclamation of Hos 12:6. Here, although the vocabulary is different, the form and the meaning are exact: יהוה אֱלֹהֵי הַצְּבָאוֹת יהוה זִכְרוֹ. Then see Ex 3:15 for the equivalence of זִכְרוֹ and שְׁמוֹ.

It is evident that there is a very strong relation between v 3 of the Song and these acclamations found in the prophets. All

of the instances discussed above are doxologies. The widely
held opinion concerning the texts in Amos and Hosea is that
they belong to the late redaction for adaptation to the cult[15].
The instance where the whole form is present, Jer 33:2, is
post-exilic and a cult interpolation[16]. This then confirms that
the liturgical formulas in the Song are of the type in use by
psalmic composers who considered themselves successors to
the prophets and who wrote the Song for redactional placement
in its present position in the Pentateuch and to convert the
preceding material to cult use.

It is of interest to note that Jer 33:2, the one instance of the
exact form of this doxology, is an interjection into a passage
that proclaims the post-exilic rebuilding of the walls of Jerusalem
destroyed by the Babylonian army, see vv 4-9. V 4 indicates the
houses that had to be torn down so as to strengthen the walls,
and by v 8 they are rebuilt by God. The cult redaction of Jer 33
is related to the post-exilic Levitical singers because of the
presence of the הוֹדוּ refrain in v 11[17]. It is also related to the
wider sphere of post-exilic Levitical redaction in general because
of the presence of the Levitical messianic additions in vv 18,
21b, 22b[18]. Thus, the same marks that we have seen constantly
regarding the opening verses, Levitical presence and the concern
for the rebuilding project, appear in the Jer 33:2 taken within
its context.

General conclusion regarding vv 1b-3, 18, 21b

All of the material has a very strong tie to a cult style that
was restricted to the post-exile and that flourished around the

---

15 Lindblom 117, 284f, 289.
16 Robert P. Carroll, *Jeremiah: A Commentary*, The Old Testament Library
    (Philadelphia: Westminster, 1986) 634-636.
17 Carroll 635.
18 Carroll 639.

time of Nehemiah and his project to rebuild the walls. Such texts are Is 12:1-6; 25:1, 9; 26:1f; Is 63:1; Ps 48:15; Ps 118; Neh 9:18; Jer 33:2. The formulas were for use in processions into the temple or city of Jerusalem: Is 12:1-6; 25:1, 9; 26:1f; 63:1; Ps 48; 118; 24:7-10; 68:5. Also Neh 9:18 describes a procession.

All of the material was used by late redactors within the cult, especially the redactors of the prophets who were converting the prophetic writing for cult use: Is 12:1-6; 25:1, 9; 26:1f; Am 5:8; 9:6; Hos 12:6; Jer 33:2.

All of formulas that compose these verses are late in all of their appearances. All of the material falls within the sphere of the Levites of the second temple: Ps 118; Jer 33:2.

It can be concluded that the Song of the Sea was written for the purpose of insertion into the prose text of the Pentateuch by Levitical redactors who wished to convert the story of the exodus to cult use. It was written as a processional and at the time of the rebuilding of the walls by Nehemiah. These latter conclusions are verified within the Song itself because it speaks of a procession into the sanctuary, which is a building constructed by God, Ex 15:17.

Separate Treatment of the Refrain, vv 1b, 21b

A very large number of critics maintain that this refrain is extremely early, perhaps the earliest recorded piece of poetry in the Old Testament. This is held, of course, by those who place the whole poem in a very early period. It is also embraced by most critics who place the Song sometime later. They consider that the refrain is something much earlier, and very prestigious works have even maintained that this verse was written by an eyewitness to the sea crossing event. But there is nothing to support that position. In fact the only argument ever offered, that a short acclamation is archaic, a notion which is unacceptable in itself, rests on the presupposition that v 21b existed separately, but neither has proof that v 21b ever existed separately ever been offered.

The situation that faces the reader is that the Song presents v 1b as a hymnic intention to praise which acts as the first line of the Song. It is in the first person because the soloist uses the first person for the whole introductory confessional section. The refrain of 21b is the first line repeated, but in refrain form, that is, as an invitation to praise. That is the picture that presents itself to the reader; if the exegete maintains that it is otherwise, then it is up to him or her to present proof to the effect, and hard evidence has been wanting.

In fact, the evidence is all counter. The liturgical formulas within the Song, that is, the whole of the formulaic enclosure including the formulas of the opening lines and the refrain are clearly from the same cultic setting. The redactive texts from Is and Ps 118 embrace both the refrain and the other liturgical formulas as standard usages within their own milieu.

Moreover, there is nothing about the particular formulation of the refrain that is primitive; in fact, everything in it is of late usage. The intention to praise אָשִׁירָה לַיהוה appears in both older and recent texts, but the refrain form, the invitation to praise, שִׁירוּ לַיהוה, v 21b, appears 14 times, all in late texts: exilic, Is 42:10, or post-exilic, Jer 20:13; Ps 33:3; 68:5, 33; 96:1, 1, 2; 98:1; 105:2; 149:1; 1 Chr 16:9, 23.

The root גאה appears as a noun throughout the Old Testament, but its use as a verb is rare and restricted to late texts: Ezk 47:5 (either exilic or post-exilic), Jb 8:11; 10:16 (post-exilic).

The verb רמה appears elsewhere twice--once in an exilic text, Jer 4:29, and once in a post-exilic text, Ps 78:9.

The above indicators do not have the value of proof. It could be accidental that these word forms have not survived from an earlier period. But much more serious is the fact that the theory of very early dating of the refrain meets with an historical objection resting on the phrase סוּס וְרֹכְבוֹ, horse and its rider. The formulation cannot be reasonably interpreted except as mounted horsemen, and these are clearly participants in the battle, because they are the ones Yahweh defeats by casting them into the sea. We are speaking of cavalry.

Now in the ancient Near East at a very early period men did ride horses, but not in battle. The first record of armed horsemen appears at the bas reliefs at Tell Halaf at the beginning of the 9th century. The Assyrians began to employ them at about that time to chase the fleeing enemy or as couriers. Such is the basic picture in the pre-exile. The actual use of cavalry formations as key units in bettle seems to have been a characteristic of the Persian and period. Now the refrain presents the throwing of the cavalry into the sea as the high point of the battle and God's stroke of victory. Thus the refrain should be traced to a period when cavalry were of critical importance, thus not till the Persian period[19].

In addition, cavalry was never used by either the Egyptians or the Israelites. The first mention of it is a D text reporting the invasion of Sennacherib in the time of Hezekiah, 2 Kg 18:23. This text transmits the fact that the Assyrians considered the Israelites to be ignorant of the technique of riding war horses. The knowledge of cavalry is from contact with the East[20].

---

19 H. Weippert, "Pferd und Streitwagen," *Biblisches Reallexikon*, ed. Kurt Galling (Tubingen: J. C. B. Mohr, 1977) 254ff.
20 De Vaux, *Institutions* 224.

Furthermore, the Israelites were in rather close contact with Egyptian culture throughout their history. The psalmist cannot have them in mind when he is speaking because the Egyptians never used cavalry. The notion of defeat of cavalry must bring to mind the East for the Israelite. The Sea crossing event has already become a stylized type for this writer. In the telling of the exodus story he employs language that was of common usage to describe the defeat of a power from the East. This equivalence of the exodus with the deliverance from some eastern power does not appear before Dt-Is and his description of the return.

Many critics have sought to save the theory of early dating by changing the reading to סוּס וְרִכְבּוֹ, horse and its chariot, because chariotry was in use in Egypt from very early times[21]. But this is done without any support in the textual evidence. The reading appears in both vv 1b and 21b, where, although the refrain has already been altered by the authors to fit its cultic context, the same reading has been retained. Both verses appear to be perfectly preserved, and both have the Masoretic vowel readings affirmed by all the versions.

The emendation is then justified by its proponents through recourse to inference from the comparative method. The phrase רִכְבּוֹ is standard for use in the exodus event. Within the text itself, v 19 can be cited in support: סוּס פַּרְעֹה בְּרִכְבּוֹ, see also Ex 14:23; Dt 11:4. But in these texts "his chariotry" refers to Pharaoh, they are Pharaoh's chariots. All other occurrences of this type have a similar meaning. However, the expression that is proposed for Ex 15:1b, 21b would indicate that the chariot pertains to the horse, "horse and its chariot." This expression makes very little sense as a description of the tandem horse and chariot. A single horse with its chariot is not a possible

21 Cross, "Canaanite Myth" 127; Freedman, "Strophe and Meter" 195.

description because the chariots were drawn by multiple horses. Neither the proposed phrase nor anything similar carrying this meaning ever appears in the Scripture.

But the specific formula, "horse and its rider," does appear four other times, Jb 39:18; Jer 51:21; Hag 2:22; Zech 12:4. All the texts are definitely describing war horses and their riders, all of these texts are post-exilic[22], and except for the Jb text, all describe God's action against the great military powers of the later periods, that is, the powers from the East.

The present reading obviously is to be maintained. The proposed change is only to save the theory and without any support in evidence and is to be rejected as illicit.

The general conclusion regarding the refrain is that everything about it affirms late dating and a composition that is integral with the rest of the Song.

---

22 Carroll 841 dates Jer 51:21 very probably after the fall of Babylon.

CHAPTER FOUR
EXEGESIS OF PART ONE, VV 4-12

The Song of the Sea
within the Development of the Reed Sea Tradition

The points of contact between the Song and the traditions of
the sea crossing which are found in Ex 14 are fairly numerous[1].
The motif of the wind that controls the waters that eventually
destroy the Egyptians, vv 8, 10, must be related to Ex 14:21aβ
in which the wind motif is found. And the events following the
wind must be somehow related to the event in 27aβ. These are
the only two places in Scripture where the wind motif in the
exodus is found. Kohata identifies this verse as coming from a
redactor of J. I note that while the motif of the wind is present,
there is no real relation of specific vocabulary and phrasing
between these two passages.

However Ex 14:7 has a strong relationship of special vocabulary to v 4 of the Song, מִבְחַר שָׁלִשָׁיו. Kohata ascribes 14:7 to a
redactive level which he has identified and which is very closely
allied with the Deuteronomistic redactors[2]. Likewise the use
of מַרְכְּבֹת, v 4, relates to the same verse, 14:7, for these are the
only two places where the term is used in an exodus account.
This is also from the Deuteronomistic sounding redactors[3].

---

1   In the subsequent analysis I follow the treatment in Fujiko Kohata,
    Jahwist und Priesterschrift in Exodus 3-14, Beihefte zur Zeitschrift für
    die alttestamentliche Wissenschaft 166 (Berlin: de Gruyter, 1986). He
    has elaborated on the basic system originally found in Noth and many
    modern commentators.
2   284, 287, 294.
3   Kohata 287.

But the whole of the phrase of v 4 is מַרְכְּבֹת פַּרְעֹה וְחֵילוֹ, and חֵיל is always P. The word pair פַּרְעֹה וְחֵילוֹ is reminiscent of the P expression found in Ex 14:4, 9, 17, 28[4].

The phrase אֶרְדֹּף אַשִּׂיג, I will pursue, I will overtake, is obviously related to the sequence of events in P, Ex 14:8f[5], which is the only other place where this word pair is used in describing the exodus. The destruction of the Egyptians is depicted as a covering of the waters, vv 5, 10, and כסה in Ex 14 is P.

To summarize, the Song as a whole demonstrates no language similarity to what is found in the original J and E renditions. It has some contact with the vocabulary of P, but the strongest relation of special terms is found in its contacts with the source of a Deuteronomistic type.

There is, though, no real similarity of phrasing to any of the sources present in Ex 14. We can be more precise and state that in terms of phrasing there is no real relationship to three of them, J, E, or P, anywhere in Scripture.

However, it can be seen that the whole sweep of the wind sea events in the Song bears a strong relationship to the P redacted text of Ex 14. In the Song the action of the wind in v 8 causes the waters to stand up in heap; in 14:21a, the wind blows, and in 22b, the waters stand up. In v 9 the Song depicts the Egyptians pursuing the Israelites into the standing waters; in Ex 14:23 the Egyptians go after the Israelites who had already gone into the standing waters, 14:22, see also 14:28, 29. Also the final outcome of God's action by the wind on the water results in the Egyptians being covered by the sea, v 10a of the Song, which also occurs in Ex 14:28. This sweep of events is

---

4   Kohata 293f.

5   Noth 105f maintains that these verses are P, except for 9aα, which is J, but despite the repetition more recent commentators hold that all the material is P vocabulary; Hyatt 148, Kohata 279.

only related in the Song and in Ex 14. Thus, these two texts cannot be simply independent of each other.

The problem that results is that the Song has no specific relationship of phrasing to any of the sources as they are present in Ex 14; yet it does seem to relate the vocabulary and to the ideas as well as to the succession of events as related in the redacted text of Ex 14 as a whole.

To explain this situation I first note that where it does have an undeniable relation of vocabulary it is most strongly connected to the Deuteronomistic source in Ex 14, and then less markedly to P as well. I than continue by noting that everything that the Song has in common with P it also has in common with Deuteronomistic redactive texts found within the D corpus. The material, even in vocabulary, will demonstrate its Deuteronomistic roots over against the P formulation,

Then, when we look at phrasing, a close investigation shows that the Song demonstrates a mentality and language usage that is in a direct line with the Deuteronomistic tradition development. By this I do not mean that it is within the same period as the development of the Deuteronomistic tradition. It is to be placed within the post-Deuteronomic development of this material and theology as practiced by the Levites of the post-exilic cult of the second temple. When phrasing appears outside the Song, it will only be in these Levitical compositions.

Compare these phrases about the the waters covering the Egyptians:

הַיָּם וַיְכַסֵּהוּ	Js 24:7
כִּסָּמוֹ יָם	Ex 15:10
כִּסָּה הַיָּם	Ps 78:53
וַיְכַסּוּ מַיִם	Ps 106:11
הַמַּיִם וַיְכַסּוּ	Ex 14:28

The tradition concerning the covering of the Egyptians first appears in a post-Deuteronomic text of the Levitical redactors, Js 24:7[6]. Ps 78 and 106 are both of Levitical provenience. Ps 78 is of the Levitical clan of Asaph, Ps 78:1; and Ps 106 is of the Levitical composers because it has their chant, Ps 106:1. Both works are of the second temple (for Ps 78 see pp 152-160). Thus, the theme was developed by the Levites and entered into their cult renditions of the Reed Sea event. It has also entered the traditions of the P writer, who ultimately must be basing himself on the Levite redactors. Therefore, the same development can be seen here that was seen regarding the traditions that entered v 19 of the prose framework, traditions that were passed on by the Levites and which underwent a parallel development by P and by the Levites, who continued to develop their own traditions.

The closest correlation to what could be considered phrasing appears in Ps 78. The Song diverges from the formulation of P by its use of יָם instead of מַיִם. Thus, as much as very short expressions can, the formulations of the Song give indication of the mentality of the tradition development of the Levites emanating from Deuteronomistic traditions.

The expression, "I will pursue, I will overtake," v 9, has a correspondence to Ex 14:9. This is the only instance where there is any correlation to the Song that is restricted to P. The notion of overtaking the Israelites in the relating of the Reed Sea event only appears in the Song and P, but the tradition about pursuing the Israelites does appear in the Deuteronomistic and post-Deuteronomic redactors, Dt 11:4; Js 24:6.

Then to be noted is that יָם־סוּף as the place of the sea event, v 4 of the Song, is not proper to the J, E or P traditions.

---

6   Mayes, *Story* 51f.

It occurs nowhere in Ex 14. If the reading of יָם־סוּף in Ex 13:18a is original to the E text, then the direction given refers to the road to the Gulf of Aqabah, and is just a general indication of the turning to the south and east, see Nb 14:25; Dt 1:40[7]. What is more probable, though, is that this is an addition because דֶּרֶךְ הַמִּדְבָּר stands better, grammatically, alone[8]; compare the syntax again to Nb 14:25; Dt 1:40. Also, v 13:18b is certainly an addition because the mention of turning back to avoid war is not consonant with mention of the Israelites being in armed formation in their ascent from Egypt. The phrase used there is found elsewhere only in the late Deuteronomistic historian, see Js 1:14; 4:12. So that if יָם־סוּף is an addition, it can be presumed to be based in the Deuteronomistic tradition stream.

Neither does the P source material associate the crossing with יָם־סוּף. The P itinerary in Nb 33:8-10[9] explicitly separates the crossing in the midst of the Sea from יָם־סוּף.

The P redactor of Ex 13-16 does, however, acknowledge the location of the miracle as being יָם־סוּף, but in such a way that it becomes clear that it is not part of his own tradition. If the P redacted itinerary of Ex 13:20; 14:2; 15:22, 23, 27; 16:1[10] is compared with Nb 33:6-11, one can see that they agree exactly for all stations except that the יָם־סוּף station, which is found between Elim and Midbar Sin in Nb 33:10, is not found there in Ex 16:1. Instead, there is simply the statement that the congregation of Israel moved. But it does appear in 14:2b, 9; 15:22. Compare:

---

7   De Vaux, *Early History* 1:377.
8   De Vaux, *Early History* 1:377, 384.
9   De Vaux, *Early History* 1:334, Philip J. Budd, *Numbers*, Word Biblical Commentary 5 (Waco: Word Book, 1984) 350.
10 Source criticism follows Hyatt, *Exodus* 148, 171, 173.

Ex 13:20	J	Succoth	Nb 33:6	Succoth
	J	Ethan		Ethan
14:2	P	Pi Hahiroth	7	Pi Hahiroth
	P	Migdol		Baal Zaphon
	P	Baal Zaphon		Migdol
Ex 14f		cross the sea	8	cross the sea
15:22a	**P**	**leave סוּף־יָם**		**no mention of סוּף יָם**
	P	Midbar Shur		Midbar
15:22b	J	three days journey		three days journey
		to the desert		to the desert of Ethan
v 23	J	Marah		Marah
15:27	P	Elim	v 9	Elim
16:1	**P**	**formula**	v 10	סוּף יָם

The difference can only be explained by the fact that the P editor of Ex 14-16 has changed the itinerary of his own tradition. It is very reasonable that someone would alter the order of the itinerary to make the יָם־סוּף station conform to an established tradition that the Sea crossing took place there. The reverse would not be possible, because it would mean that someone has wanted to consciously separate the crossing from יָם־סוּף and so deny a now-established tradition.

Moreover, when the editor gets to where the יָם־סוּף station originally was placed, Ex 16:1, he uses a filler, "all the congregation of the Sons of Israel," a formula to fill up what is missing, to replace the station that he lifted out and shifted to the sea crossing.

Also, Ex 14:2, 9 is the only place where the P editor of Ex 13-16 in his own material talks about encampment, but the list of Nb 33 has the encampment theme as part of its own proper language, 33:5-14 passim. So that the language of Ex 14 regarding the encampment is borrowed. Compare:

Nb 33:11 וַיִּסְעוּ מִיַּם־סוּף   Nb 33:10 וַיַּחֲנוּ עַל־יַם־סוּף

Ex 14:2 תַחֲנוּ עַל־הַיָּם

Ex 15:22 וַיַּסַּע ... מִיַּם־סוּף   Ex 14:9 חֹנִים עַל־הַיָּם

The indication is that the editor has taken the יַם־סוּף station of Nb 33:10 and lifted it whole, including its attendant language, and used it as part of the crossing scene. The language concerning the camping is derived from the itinerary list of Nb 33 or one like it, where it originally had nothing to do with a miracle.

The P tradition itself places the crossing at Pi Hahiroth, Nb 33:8, which it does not identify with the יַם־סוּף encampment, Nb 33:10. The P editor of Ex 14 retains his own tradition that the crossing was at Pi Hahiroth, Ex 14:2, but also acknowledges the tradition that the crossing was at יַם־סוּף by combining the two encampments. What is clear is that the identification of יַם־סוּף with the crossing is not proper to P but a legitimate tradition that he has accepted from another source.

None of the material of the J, E or P sources ever makes the identification[11]. On the other hand the D source always makes the identification, Dt 11:4; Js 2:10; 4:23; 24:6. It is the latest level of the Deuteronomistic historical redactors and the post-Deuteronomists in which this identification first appears. This יַם־סוּף crossing tradition then only appears in works that are post-Deuteronomic and demonstrate heavy D influence, Neh 9:9; Ps 106:7, 9, 22; 136:13, 15. These are compositions done within the ambit of the second temple. They are all from the Levitical cult personnel, Neh 9 explicitly so, see 9:4f. Ps 136, like the already discussed Ps 106, can be identified with the Levites because of the Levitical chant, in 136:1. Thus, whether in prose or poetry, the יַם־סוּף tradition as the place of the miracle has a strict and unique relation to the Levites.

---

11 Hyatt, *Exodus* 149, 158.

The use of the P elements for pharaoh's army, פַּרְעֹה חֵיל, v 4a, is first present in the exilic Deuteronomistic historian, Dt 11:3, 4. But the specific phrasing that the Song uses in the destruction scene in Ex 15:4 is only found elsewhere in the Levitical Ps 136.

Ex 15:4		Ps 136:15
מַרְכְּבֹת (J)		
פַּרְעֹה וְחֵילוֹ (D, P)		פַּרְעֹה וְחֵילוֹ (D, P)
יָרָה בַיָּם (J concept)		נִעֵר ... בְיַם־ (J)
בְיַם־סוּף (D)		סוּף (D)

Ps 136 shows overall P influences. The description of the creation of the sun and moon, vv 6-9, are very close to the P account of creation, Gn 1:16. The description of the Reed Sea event is also very close to the P redacted account. Ps 136:14, 15 can be compared to Ex 14:27b, 28. It is of the second temple because of its very close agreement with P and because God is described as the God of heaven, v 26, a title characteristic of the Persian period[12]. What is of import is to note that a second temple composition comes up with what is basically the same construction usage that is found in the Song. Nor does the text admit to be called a quotation of the Song. It has, rather, the characteristic of free use of historical traditions according to a current liturgical manner. And again, the history of the usage is Levitical in its origins.

The standing of the waters in v 8aβ is found virtually intact in a second temple Levitical psalm, the Asaphite Ps 78:13. מַיִם replaces נֹזְלִים, but מַיִם is the equivalent of נֹזְלִים in the parallelism of v 8 of the Song. The indication is, again, of a sphere of usage:

---

12 Ravasi 3:731.

Ex 15:8 ...מַיִם נִצְבוּ כְמוֹ־נֵד נֹזְלִים

Ps 78:13 וַיַּצֶּב־מַיִם כְּמוֹ־נֵד

Moreover, it can be shown that the derivation of both these texts is ultimately traceable to D. The notion that the waters stood up like a נֵד, a dike, is found elsewhere only in the account of the Jordan River crossing, Js 3:13, 16. We have already seen that it is the Deuteronomistic redactor who makes the River and Sea traditions equal, Js 4:23, so that the description of the Jordan River crossing can be applied to the Reed Sea tradition. In so doing he also allows that the standing of the waters, which permitted the Israelites to cross the Jordan, could be applied to the crossing of the Reed Sea. But that application does not appear until after the Deuteronomistic redactor.

The standing of the waters of the Reed Sea does not appear in any early tradition. The J and E traditions are unaware of any such concept. Nor does the tradition appear in any D text; even as late as the Deuteronomistic historian. The Deuteronomistic confession of Dt 11:3f has no trace of a standing of the water tradition. Even the post-Deuteronomic Js 24 is makes no mention of it; see 24:5-7. Even Js 24:3 itself, although it makes the two events, the Sea and the River, equal and talks of a crossing, does not as yet explicitly speak of a standing of the waters; it only makes such a formulation possible. Because the Jordan stood, and the Jordan and the Reed Sea or equivalent events, it will be possible to arrive at a standing of the sea. Such an idea does appear, but only in the epoch of the second temple. Thus, this tradition appears to be post-Deuteronomic. It has also been taken over from the Levites by P and formulated according to P's own development, Ex 14:22, 29.

Again, the origin and development is to be found in the Levites, and the form in which it appears in the Song with the use of נֵד is restricted to these Levitical circles. The Song text itself has to be Levitical and post-Deuteronomic because it is beyond the development of the Deuteronomistic schools. The very close conformity that the Song phrase has with the Levitical Ps 78:13 confirms this.

We can reach an overall conclusion concerning the place of the Song in the development of the Reed Sea tradition. It consistently demonstrates a Deuteronomistic influence, but is post-Deuteronomic and Levitical.

The problem of the Song's relation to P has to be resolved in the same way that the prose explanation's relation to P was. The formulaic enclosure shows that it was written in Jerusalem, in the post-exile, and for placement in the Pentateuch after Ex 14. The version of the Pentateuch would have been the P redacted one that came with Ezra, so that the writers would know the P redacted text of Ex 14.

The Song has another phrase that is involved in the development of the Reed Sea tradition. It does not emanate from D, but it is found in a Levitical second temple work. V 5b, is found as an exact duplicate in Neh 9:11b. Also the end phrase of Neh 9:11b, can be compared with the ending of the parallel phrase to v 5b of the Song, v 10b. Again we have the indication that we are in a cultic milieu of usage.

There is additional evidence that precludes the notion that Neh 9:11 is a quotation of a much earlier work. Compare the following texts:

		תַּשְׁלִיכֵנִי מְצוּלָה	Jon 2:4
		תַּשְׁלִיךְ בִּ מְצֻלוֹת	Mic 7:19b
הִשְׁלַכְתָּ בִּ מְצוֹלוֹת ; כְּמוֹ־אֶבֶן בְּמַיִם עַזִּים			Neh 9:11
יָרְדוּ בִ מְצוֹלֹת כְּמוֹ־אָבֶן ;			Ex 15:5
כְּ... בְּמַיִם אַדִּירִים			Ex 15:10

In both the Song text of 15:5 and the Neh text I have used a semicolon to indicate the break in the hemistichs. I have done this to show that if Neh 9:11 is quoting from the Song of the Sea, he would have to have taken a hemistich from the song's poetry and divided it so that it appeared in two hemistichs in Neh 9:11. That is possible, but not likely if one is quoting or remembering a long established poetic pattern.

Also, Neh 9:11 appears to be using an expression of his time to depict destruction. The Micah text is usually dated to the early post-exile[13] as is the one in Jonah[14]. Thus, it is reasonable to assume that Neh 9:11 is employing current expressions. If he were quoting the line from the Song as from an ancient work, and at the same time using an expression of his day, he would, in essence, be quoting מצלה twice. That is again possible, but it is not a natural explanation of events. Overall, it is very difficult to explain the relationship of the texts as one of quotation. The real indication here is that the passages of both the Song and Neh 9 each reflect current use within a cultic milieu and a period.

Support for the notion that we are simply confronted with two passages from a late period comes from the fact that צול appears only in late passages. It appears 11 times outside the Song and never before the exile: Is 44:27; Jon 2:4; Mic 7:19; Zech 1:8; 10:11; Jb 41:23; Ps 68:23; 69:3, 16; 88:7; 107:24; Neh 9:11. An argument can be made against Ps 68:23, but it is difficult to speak of God bringing back from Bashan, and thus

---

13 James L. Mays, *Micah*, Old Testament Library (London: SCM, 1976) 155, 167f.

14 John. D. W. Watts dates it after the return and not later than the reform of Ezra; *The Books of Joel, Obadiah, Jonah, Nahum, Habakkuk and Zephanaiah* (Cambridge: Cambridge University Press, 1975) 84-86. Giuseppi Bernini, *Sofonia - Gioele - Abdia - Giona*, Nuovissima Versione della Bibbia (Roma: Paoline, 1972) 240. It is post-exilic for sure and most likely from the fifth or fourth centuries.

from the North, without it having the connotation of the restoration from exile.

Thus, all of the Reed Sea depiction shows that the Song belongs to the development of that tradition as carried out by the cult Levites in the second temple.

Verse by Verse Analysis of the Reed Sea Section

The Egyptians go down to destruction, vv 4, 5

It has been shown that v 4b definitely is related to the Deuteronomistic type text of Ex 14:7, but does not have its phrasing mentality. The only instance of such a mentality is found in the destruction of the nations literature, Jer 48:15:

$$\text{Ex 15:4b} \quad \text{וּמִבְחַר שָׁלִשָׁיו טֻבְּעוּ}$$
$$\text{Ex 15:5b} \quad \text{יְרְדוּ}$$
$$\text{Jer 48:15} \quad \text{וּמִבְחַר בַּחוּרָיו יָרְדוּ}$$

It is also interesting to note that Jer 48:14 has a correspondence to its immediate formulaic context that is very similar to Ex 15:4b, 5b and its context. Compare Jer 48:14, אֲנָשִׁי...לַמִּלְחָמָה, 48:15, שְׁמוֹ הַמֶּלֶךְ ... יהוה, with Ex 15:3 and its cognate, 15:18. The Song has a natural relation to the phrasing of this type of literature.

Texts in Ps 107 and Ezk have a general resemblance to v 5 of the Song as a whole, especially in the formula language. Ezk 31:15 and 26:19f contain the all of the formula elements: תְּהוֹם, יָרַד, כָּסָה. Ps 107:26 has the expression יֵרְדוּ תְהוֹמוֹת. But the deeps are the equivalent of the מְצוּלָה, 107:24. There results the closest instance to the phrasing mentality of the Song:

הֹמֹת ... יָרְדוּ בִמְצוֹלֹת   Ex 15:5

בִמְצוּלָה   Ps 107:24

יֵרְדוּ   Ps 107:26

תְּהוֹמוֹת

Ps 107 is from the Levitical cult singers because of the presence of the chant in 107:1[15]. The Levitical phrasing here and in the above mentioned Ps 136:15 and Neh 9:11b covers virtually all of vv 4 and 5. The whole of the phrasing is comprised of formulations from the Levites and the post-exilic redactor of Jeremiah. This combination of Levitical material and material that bears a strong resemblance to the late redactors of the prophets, and which then simply defines a block of material in the Song, is something that appeared in vv 1-3, and then will reappear with frequency in the Song.

The exaltation of God's right hand, v 6

Within the Scriptures, v 6, in its phrasing, bears closest resemblance to Ps 118:15b, 16, whose Levitical and post-exilic nature has been discussed above. It has the description of Yahweh's right hand repeated followed by laudatory phrases denoting its exaltation and power. The technique of repeating a power attribute of Yahweh cannot be a borrowing by Ps 118 from the Song; it is his own proper style. Compare the triple repetition of the right hand of Yahweh with the triple repetition of the name of Yahweh in 118:10-12. Thus, in terms of poetic phrasing, vocabulary and style, the line relates to the Levitical sphere.

---

15 Walter Beyerlin, *Werden und Wesen des 107 Psalms*, Beihefte zur Zeitschrift für die alttestamentliche Wissenschaft 153 (Berlin: de Gruyter, 1979) 102-106.

A note on the mythological character of the Song

It has already been noted that v 6 corresponds to mythological notions about the empowering of the deity for his victory over the waters. The full extent of the similarity between v 6 and KTU 1.2, IV, 8f, has already been discussed above (pp 35f). The similarity to the Akkadian text is also striking:

Enuma elish IV, 16[16]: Your weapons shall not fail;
    they   shall smash your foes!
Ex 15:6: your right hand, Yahweh, is exalted in power,
    your right hand, Yahweh, shall smash the foe.

The correspondence is yet closer when another line describing the weapon of Marduk is taken into account and compared to the description of the "power" of Yahweh's right hand in the Song's text:

III, 52: the Power Weapon so potent in its sweep.

The Akkadian text, like its Ugaritic counterpart, appears as the empowerment of the deity before his victory over the sea. Such a positioning corresponds to the Song, where the defeat of the enemy immediately follows, vv 7ff. Thus, there are definite points of contact with both the Ugaritic and Akkadian myth accounts.

V 6, though, is only the first of a number of places in the Song where there are definite traces of the influence of myth. This correspondence is to both the Akkadian and Ugaritic systems, and the correspondence is not just to individual vocabulary, phrasing and concepts, but to the myth systems as a whole.

---

16 The translation of the Enuma elish is from *Ancient Near Eastern Texts*, 3rd ed., James B. Pritchard ed. (Princeton: Princeton UP, 1969).

The scope of events in the Song can be compared to both myth systems:

KTU 1.2, IV 8f; Enuma elish IV, 16: The power of the deity against his enemy, the sea, is proclaimed immediately before his victory.

Ex 15:6: The power of Yahweh is proclaimed against his enemy immediately before his victory over them in the sea.

KTU 1.2, IV, 11-40; Enuma elish IV: The deity defeats his enemy, the waters, and gains control of them.

Ex 15:8: Yahweh defeats his enemies by the waters that he controls.

KTU 1.4, VII, 49f; Enuma elish VII, 13f: The deity, after his victory, is supreme among the gods.

Ex 15:11a: Yahweh, after he has worked his victory, is declared incomparable among the gods.

KTU 1.3,4; Enuma elish VI, 51-74: The deity builds a sanctuary for his residence.

Ex 15:17: Yahweh has built a sanctuary for his residence.

KTU 1.2, IV, 10, 32; Enuma elish IV, 27: The deity is acclaimed king.

Ex 15:18: Yahweh is acclaimed to rule as king.

The Song of the Sea cannot be termed a strictly mythological account; rather it uses myths to portray the historical saving events of exodus and conquest. In doing so, it has demythologized those elements that have entered into the work. But it indicates that the author knows the mythology of the surrounding cultures and has absorbed them to such an extent that he could use them with ease. The period of usage of the myth forms in the Song has to be ascertained by the examination of each instance within its context in the Scriptures.

God's anger is dispatched, v 7

The formulaic language is of the type that expresses Yahweh's anger against those who seek to resist him. It does not easily separate itself from the previous verse, which expresses his power against the foe, and the following verse, which expresses his anger in the enactment of the standing of the waters. In terms of general vocabulary the texts with major correspondences are Is 5:24f, against Israel, and more so, the poem added to the oracles of Nahum describing God's anger against an enemy nation, Nah 1:1-11; see vv 6a and especially 10b. Both the Is[17] and Nah[18] text are of the post-exilic redactors to the prophets

But in terms of actual phrasing and overall mentality the line bears a definite resemblance to the text of Ps 78:49. The word pair שָׁלַּח חָרוֹן, send fury, appears only in these two texts. Ps 78 also predicates the phrase of God, against the Egyptians, and in the context of the exodus in general. But beyond this single correspondence, the whole of v 7 and the beginning of v 8 show a narrative mentality that is similar to that of Ps 78. The Song has a series of quasi-personified attributes of God that he uses to destroy the enemy: the greatness of his majesty, his fury, and in v 8a the breath of his anger. Ps 78:49 also has a multiplication of anger terms that are quasi-personified: the heat of his anger, fury, indignation, and trouble. These are personified to the point where they are called a deputation of messengers of evils.

Thus all of v 7 falls into the usages of post-exilic redactors to the prophets and the Levites of the same period. But phrasing

17 Kaiser, *Isaiah 1-12* 99.
18 A summary of the current theories of the redaction of the Nahum psalm can be found in Otto Kaiser, *Einleitung in des Alte Testament 5* (Gütersloh: Gerd Mohn, 1984) 242f. He places the critical v 10 among the additions to the psalm.

and style is limited to the piece from the school of Asaph, Ps 78:49. V 7 is the first instance where the major idea or key usage is found elsewhere only in the work of the Asaphites. This virtually exclusive tie to the Asaphite mentality continues through every verse until v 17, without exception.

The standing of the waters, v 8

In v 8 there begins the actual description of God's handling of the waters at the sea. The phrasing is of the order of a cosmic myth transposition of the event's narration. The phrase רוּחַ אַפֶּיךָ, the breath or wind of your nostrils, is a description of the wind at the Reed Sea event which controls the waters. In the J redactor's account it is certainly God who is behind the event of the east wind, but the wind is what he sends to accomplish his purpose. The Song of the Sea, however, uses an anthropomorphism. It describes this wind as the breath of God, putting God into direct control of the waters. The use of wind to control the waters puts this passage into the general category of the God of the storm. The phrase also expresses the fierce anger of God, the term אַף indicating both nostrils and anger. The waters that he uses are termed תְּהֹום, the primordial abyss. So the passage uses motifs of the struggle between the chaotic waters and deity, who uses the tools of the storm to defeat them and thereby gain control of them. It is thus allied to the Near Eastern myth system where the initial victory is accomplished by the storm, and thereafter there is order in the universe. Baal, who is lord of the storm, defeats Yam-Nahar with the tools of the storm, KTU 1.2, IV, 8-40; 1.3, C, 23. Also Marduk defeats Tiamat with use primarily of the wind, Enuma elish IV, 30-146. תְּהֹמת, v 8, the term used to indicate the waters that have come under God's control, is simply a form of Tiamat.

The portrayal in the Song is historicized and demythologized. Although the motif of the water struggle can still be recognized, it has been used to portray the wind that blew over the sea at the exodus. The notion of the primordial struggle against the waters has been applied to an act of God in history in which he destroys the enemy nation and saves his people.

The specific usage of the breath of God's nostrils that is an anthropomorphism that depicts his control of the waters and which enacts deliverance for his chosen one, appears as salvation for the individual in Ps 18:16f, a psalm whose dating is disputed (but see p 115 below).

The term אף also appears in passages where Yahweh's anger against the waters is used to portray the historical salvation of the people and the destruction of the enemy nation, Hab 3, especially vv 8, 12. Hab 3 has been subject to a dating procedure that compares it to Ugaritic literature and which has dated it to a very early period of Israelite history, sometime during the period of the Judges. But this dating method has not been proven valid (see pp 116-119). Critics who do not belong to this school normally take into account that the text is an addition to the late pre-exilic prophet and can be presumed to be from the same time period as the composition of the rest of the work or a later composition. J. Lindblom places its among the prophets who are also temple personnel of the time immediately before the exile. The most probable assumption is that the enemy it has in mind is the Babylonians[19].

In the placement of the Song's text, the first thing I note is that myth forms are never applied to the exodus until the exilic and post-exilic periods. The earliest such application is Dt-Isaian, Is 51:9f. The writer uses the motif of the primordial monsters, 51:9, who in myth imagery, are convertible with the chaotic

---

19 Lindblom 254.

waters, 51:10a. There is no explicit mention of the exodus, but it can be presumed to be present in the author's mind because he speaks of the days of long ago, 51:9, and then of the drying of the sea and the Israelites passing through it, 51:10.

In arriving at these formulations he adds myth forms to texts that are a development or restatement of his own themes. The drying of the sea in 51:10a is a continuation of 44:27a. The road in the waters for the redeemed appears first as a description of the way for the returnees, 43:2, who are the redeemed of 43:1b. It takes on an exodus connotation in 43:16, whose vocabulary can be compared to all of 51:10. This action is described as something done of old, 51:9, which can be compared with the description of the placing of the road in the waters as one of the things of old, 43:18. He has taken his own water texts, that are not of a visibly mythical nature, and which he has previously used to depict the return or used in portraying the return as the new exodus, and developed them with the use of myth forms. Dt-Is does not present itself as having a pattern of an earlier tradition of myth description of the Reed Sea event. He builds from within his own work and from myth formulations current in his day.

The other texts where myth forms are still visible in their portrayal of the Reed Sea event are Ps 74:13-15; 77:17-20; 106:9. The text of Ps 74, like Isaiah itself, does not explicitly speak of the exodus; still, we can know that the Sea event is being treated. V 2 speaks about the people that God redeemed and obtained "long ago." which has to mean the act of the redemption at the beginning of Israelite history in which Yahweh obtained for himself a people, the exodus. Then in v 11 the psalmist speaks about the event of "long ago" and about the defeat of the waters and the river. It can be affirmed that he is treating the exodus.

The above psalms can all be attributed to the Sons of Asaph. Those that are affirmed as their compositions according to the headings that have been placed at their beginnings are Ps 50, 73-83. But three other can be claimed for them with some surety. In 1 Chr 16:7 the Asaphites chant in the liturgy before the ark for the first time. The psalmody is made up of Ps 105:1-15; 96; 106:1, 47f, which are found in 1 Chr 16:8-22, 23-33, 34-36 respectively. Thus it was the point of view in the post-exile that these psalms were part of the primordial repertory of the Asaphites, and it can be safely assumed that they were composed within their immediate sphere. Therefore, Ps 96, 105, 106 can be placed within their corpus.

The school as a whole continues in the line of the Dt-Isaian application of myth to the exodus. Ps 74:13f speaks of the crushing of the monsters. Though it uses a different vocabulary than that of Is 51:9, it has certainly been influenced by the Dt-Isaian text because it has the same formula to portray the myth notion. It speaks of the days of old, קֶדֶם, 74:12, and then goes on to use the repetition of אַתָּה as a stylistic technique to address God and to introduce the praise descriptions of his victory over the primordial sea monsters, vv 13a, 14a. This can be compared with the days of old, קֶדֶם, in Is 51:9, and the direct address to Yahweh's arm, הֲלוֹא אַתְּ־הִיא, that is the repeated introduction to the praise descriptions of his victory over the same monsters in 51:9b, 10a.

Also, Ps 74:15b is Dt-Isaian in sound and formulation, see Is 44:27b; 42:15. It has taken these Isaian return texts that are not of themselves mythical, or, as in the case of 44:27b, might have a myth shading, applied them to the exodus, and developed them according to a mythical mold. The Asaphites thus continue the Dt-Isaian application of return texts to the exodus and the development of the theme by the use of myth forms.

Ps 77:17-20 describes God and his actions on the waters in much the same way that Hab 3 does, except that it applies it to the exodus. But the text of Ps 77 is also in the line of the myth development that originated in Dt-Is; compare v 20 to Is 43:16; 51:10. Ps 77 therefore also continues the adaptation of Isaian material to the exodus and to the mythical model.

Ps 106:9 directs the notion of the rebuke of the waters to the crossing of the Israelites. This verse can be compared also with Is 51:10. But more clearly than in Dt-Is it a transposition to the Reed Sea of the myth statement of Is 50:2b.

So that the Asaphites are the ones who, after its beginning in Dt-Is, have carried out the application of myth to the Reed Sea event[20]. In so doing they have not limited themselves to just one myth motif, but have added various myth themes to describe different aspects of the Reed Sea event.

Thus it is in the Asaphite school, and only in the Asaphite school, that you have the same mechanics that are found in v 8 of the Song, the application of the myth description of the God of the storm to the exodus. Therefore, our text is best placed within the ambit of the Asaphites in their post-exilic development of the Reed Sea tradition for the cult.

---

20 Ps 114:3f and 66:6 have often been included in this category. Both sea and river have come under God's action, and that would indicate the presence of the myth description of the god Yam-Nahar, Sea-River, who is the foe of Baal. But it is not clear that one can speak of living myth forms. In Ps 66 the river-sea pair does not appear as more than an expression. In Ps 114 there is the notion of the waters fleeing. But the mode of speech is one where the waters are addressed directly and in the same way that the hills are addressed as skipping sheep. There is a light poetic form present, certainly nothing of the myth struggle. It is the use of myth modes in a simply stylistic way. In any case, both of the psalms are late, and both are tied to Dt-Is. For example, Ps 114:8 is Dt-Isaian in its formulation, see Is 41:18. Ps 66:6 is of comparable expression to what is found in Is 51:10f, and Ps 66:12 is very close to Is 43:2.

Beside the use of water myth in general, we already know that the phrasing of v 8aβ is Asaphite, from Ps 78:13b. But beyond this the specific vocabulary usages of our piece are tied to the same school. The Song differs from Ps 78 in that it has used נֹזְלִים to portray the waters of the Sea. The root נזל when it is used within the depiction of the exodus event in general follows the same pattern that we saw above, from the Dt-Isaian to the Asaphite school. It is used in the description of the return, Is 44:3; God promises water in the desert for his returnees. Then it describes the bringing forth of the water in the desert at the exodus, 48:21. That notion is taken over by the Asaphites, whose phrasing depends on Dt-Is, Ps 78:16. It is then also given another exodus application, the plague on the waters of the Egyptians, 78:44.

תהום to describe the waters of the Reed Sea is also Asaphite, and the pattern similar to the development traced above. It appears in Dt-Is, Is 51:10. There is then another appearance in the school of Isaiah, Is 63:13. The other occurrences are Asaphite, Ps 77:17; 106:9. Its only other use within the wider realm of the exodus tradition in general is also of their school, Ps 78:15, where it describes the waters in the desert. Thus the psalmic uses of the word to describe the exodus event are limited to the Asaphite sphere.

Therefore, in overall concept, phrasing, and vocabulary usage the line is very heavily Asaphite in nature.

The enemy's plans, v 9

The situation represented in v 9 is that the enemy says that he will dispossess the Israelites: אָמַר אוֹיֵב ... תּוֹרִישׁ The use of the verb ירשׁ to describe the notion of the enemy dispossessing the Israelites is only found elsewhere in Ezk 35:10; 36:2, and the Asaphite Ps 83:13. There is a very intense relationship between the Song text and these two texts taken together, and they may be considered together because the texts of Ps 83 and Ezk are closely tied.

Both of these texts match the overall concept of the Song in that there is the descent into the mind of the enemy who plans to do the dispossessing, and they portray it with a vocabulary that matches that of the Song. The real relation to the Ezk texts is apparent on examination, especially of 36:2, where the same vocabulary is used, אָמַר הָאוֹיֵב ...לְמוֹרָשָׁה הָיְתָה לָּנוּ. The layout of the Ezk phrase, like the Song, lets you into the mind and the actual words that the enemies use to express their plans.

The relationship of vocabulary between the Song and the text of Ps 83 is less obvious but still fully present. The psalm speaks about "those who say let us take possession for ourselves," אֲשֶׁר אָמְרוּ נִירֲשָׁה לָּנוּ. They are the same ones who let us know their plans in v 5, "They have said, Come let us cut them off" And these speakers are the enemy, אוֹיֵב, of v 3.

In addition to the vocabulary and concepts, 83:13 within its immediate context duplicates in a remarkable way the other stylistic peculiarities of v 9 of the Song. The preceding verse, Ps 83:12, has the five word alliteration formula that is found in v 9 of the Song, only using כ. Also the repeated use of the ending מוֹ is found in 83:12, 14.

We then note that there is an imprecation in the psalm addressed against the surrounding peoples, including Edom, Moab and Philistia, 83:7. The Song too is directed against the surrounding peoples who are Edom, Moab and Philistia, v 14f. And both use the relatively uncommon term פְּלֶשֶׁת to indicate the Philistines. This convergence of style and vocabulary and concept cannot be called in any way a quotation or an imitation.

It indicates living usage, and very probably, one can talk about the two texts belonging to the same school of composition.

The late dating of Ps 83 can be demonstrated with considerable certainty. It can be shown that it is not before the Ezk text and is very closely related to it. The phrasing of the two pieces have remarkable points of convergence. They both use לָנוּ to indicate dispossess for themselves. Compare Ps 83:13 to Ezk 36:2 and 35:12b. They are both against the surrounding nations who have conspired to take over the land, Ps 83:6-9; Ezk 36:5. The Ezk text makes specific mention of Edom as the primary enemy, 35:2, 15; 36:5, while Ps 83 mentions Edom as the first on the list, v 7. Both writers have the intention of making claim to land disputed with the surrounding peoples and both insist that the land of which the enemy is trying to take possession belong's to God, Ezk 35:10b; Ps 83:13. The actions of the surrounding peoples provoke the retaliation of God and result in their knowing that he is God. Ezk 35:4, 12, and Ps 83:19 can be compared:

יהוה　　וְיָדַעְתָּ כִּי־אֲנִי　　Ezk 35:12

יהוה ... וְיֵדְעוּ כִּי־אַתָּה　　Ps 83:19

They are really the same statement except that in the Ezk the prophetic pronouncement has God speaking in the first person. In Ps 83 the text continues the imprecation speech and is therefore in the second person address.

Though the texts must be strongly related, we can show that the Ezk text cannot be dependent on Ps 83. The use of אָמַר to describe the intentions of the surrounding peoples is of the speech of the writer in Ezk, 35:10a, 12a; 36:2, as is יָרַשׁ, 35:10b; 36:2, 3b; 5b. The use of לָנוּ to describe their plans is original in Ezk, 35:12b; 36:2. It also appears in 35:10a as לִי.

The saying that "someone will know that Yahweh is God" is part of the entire structure of the book of Ezekiel and its pattern of prophetic speech. In the present context and as against the surrounding nations, see 35:4b; 36:36a. The phrase appears 71 times overall in the book and is a characteristic of Ezk, probably of the redactor[21], and it is used always to close off a prophetic announcement, as it closes off the announcement of Ps 83. Ps 83 is thus copying a prophetic announcement for the entreaty liturgy.

The time of origin of the Ezk text is disputed. It really can not be placed any earlier than the late exile because it speaks of the restoration as an assured thing, 36:8-10. In fact, the Ezk passage is much better placed in the post-exile because the whole of 35:1-36:15 looks like a land dispute, something that does not become critical before the return[22]. There are a considerable group of exegetes who place the text in the first half of the fifth century, before the work of Nehemiah[23].

Whatever the case might be in regard to the text from Ezk, there is good reason to place Ps 83 in the fifth century. The psalm speaks of a conspiracy against Israel which the surrounding peoples have entered into together. They are aided in this by Assyria, vv 7-9. Various exegetes have inferred from the mention of Assyria that the psalm has to be from the pre-exile, but the inference is incorrect. The name Assyria was often used to denote the reigning power in the East that ruled over Israel long after the disappearance of the Assyrian empire, see Ezr 6:22; Is 11:11, 16; 19:23, 25; Mic 5:4, 5; 7:12; Zech 10:10f. Also see Neh 9:32, where the present period is still considered

---

21 Herbert G. May, "The Book of Ezekiel," *The Interpreter's Bible*, vol. 6 (Nashville: Abingdon, 1956) 62 col. b.

22 Walther Zimmerli, *Ezekiel 2*, trans. James D. Martin, Hermeneia (Philadelphia: Fortress, 1983) 234.

23 May 47, 259f.

the time of Assyria. Psalm 83, because it really cannot be prior to the Ezk text, must be placed sometime after the late exile, at the earliest. Machinations of the surrounding peoples where they seek the assistance of the king of the reigning power in the East, Persia, against Judah can, therefore, only be placed sometime after the return.

Opposition from the surrounding peoples occurs for the first time at the occasion of the rebuilding of the temple, Ezr 4:4f. But their actions do not seem to be the reason for the failure to rebuild the temple, nor is there any indication that the king of Persia ever entered into the dispute. The failure to rebuild was really based on the lack of initiative among the people, Hag 2:2ff, and when they did begin the rebuilding in serious, they did not have to stop the work, even while the matter was verified, Ezr 5:3-5. There is never any indication that the Persians went back on the rescript that had been given to the first returned exiles for the rebuilding of the temple; see Ezr 1:2-4; 6:3-15.

The depiction of the surrounding peoples' opposition as the reason for the delay in the rebuilding is mostly a reading back of a later situation into the temple reconstruction. The only time when Persia did support the policies of the those peoples against Judah was during the reign of Xerxes, in 486 or 485, see Ezr 4:6-23. The policy was against the rebuilding of the walls of Jerusalem, which Xerxes stopped by force of arms.

Psalm 83 represents a post-exilic time period when there had been harassment by the surrounding peoples that had obviously been successful and which was recent enough to provoke a rather violent imprecation ceremony and a plea that God reverse the situation. The only historical situation into which it can be placed is the period when there was a great desire in Israel to rebuild the walls. Judah's main center, Jerusalem, was exposed and militarily could not be defended. Without the walls, Israel was in an extremely weak military position in regard to the surrounding peoples, Ps 83:5, and left itself open to land grabbing on their part, 83:13, especially by Edom, 83:7. Ps 83 should be placed in the time when the land grabbing by the surrounding peoples was going on and when they had been successful in stopping the project to rebuild the walls.

That placement is confirmed by the following. The phrase that begins the poem, "God, do not be silent to yourself, do not be speechless, and do not be still, O God," is found elsewhere only in Is 62:1, 6, 7a, and there virtually intact. And Is 62 is also a plea introducing a cult ceremony built to imitate prophetic speech. And the plea is for the completion of the reconstruction of the walls of Jerusalem, 62:7b, 6a.

The policy of Xerxes was reversed by the rescript of Artaxerxes because of the good offices of Nehemiah, Neh 1:1-2:10. Psalm 83 should then be placed after the rescript of Xerxes in 486 stopping the rebuilding and before the success of Nehemiah in 446, when permission to rebuild was obtained.

Ex 15 depicts a very similar situation in the second part, except that God has now actually made these nations helpless and has successfully carried out the building project, vv 14-18. Thus, the Song is well placed at or after Nehemiah's successful rebuilding of the walls.

The vocabulary usage uniformly supports the late dating of this passage, and it confirms the Ezekielan and Asaphite influences that have been postulated for this line. The word pair מלא נפש, to have one's desire, gives evidence of being a late usage. It is limited to Jer 31:25; Ps 107:9; Prov 6:30; Qo 6:7. Probably all the these texts are post-exilic. The cultic texts are Ps 107:9 and Jer 31:25. The former text is from the Levitical cult singers, see their refrain in v 1. It will be shown below that this refrain was most closely identified with the Asaphites (see p 182). Jer 31:25 also falls into the Levitical and Asaphite sphere (see pp 131f).

The phrase רִיק הֶרֶב is unattested outside of Ezk and the code of holiness, which is so heavily related to Ezk, Lv 26:33; Ezk 5:2, 12; 12:14; 28:7; 30:11. The Lv text is from the exilic redaction of the code because 26:33 itself speaks of the exile. Therefore, all of the texts are exilic or later.

It seems that if we are seeking psalmic authors of this line, they must be the Asaphites in the post-exile working on a theme of the school of Ezekiel. The whole concept of the line, its phrasing and vocabulary all indicate it.

The Sea covers the Egyptians, v 10

V 10 continues the description of the destruction of the Egyptians, or rather repeats the description found in v 5. Here also it can be demonstrated that the controlling idea is Asaphite. In the psalms the two instances of the use of כסה in the description of the Reed Sea event are in Ps 106:11; 78:53, both Asaphite.

The phrase of v 10a of the Song, כִּסָּמוֹ יָם, "the sea covered them," relates the destruction of the Egyptians. In terms of simple structure its closest correlate anywhere in Scripture is Ps 78:53, כִּסָּה הַיָּם. More importantly, the two texts share the same overall formulation of the event. Ex 15:10 speaks of the sea covering "them." "Them" is a reference to the enemy, אוֹיֵב, of v 9. Thus the mentality of the author is "the sea covered them, the enemy." The full formulation of Ps 78:53 is וְאֶת־אוֹיְבֵיהֶם כִּסָּה הַיָּם, "and the sea covered their enemies." Thus the two texts are equivalent, and no other text expressing the covering of the enemy exists in Scripture. This demonstrates that not

only the phrasing is Asaphite, but the juxtaposition of vv 9 and
10 is Asaphite in conception as well.

The incomparability of Yahweh, v 11a

V 11a has also been rightly compared to formulations in the
myth stories of the struggle between the deity and the waters.
In the myth systems of the peoples of the ancient near east, the
deity, after the defeat of the waters, is able to build his sanctuary;
and then, in the assembly of the gods, he is proclaimed supreme
among the other gods. Just so, Yahweh is proclaimed supreme
בַּקֹּדֶשׁ after his defeat of the enemy by the waters. בַּקֹּדֶשׁ is
usually translated "in holiness," and perhaps justly so, and
thus it is the cult community who is proclaiming God's exaltation
in holiness over the lower celestial beings, or perhaps it is a
denial of any power and real existence to other gods. But בַּקֹּדֶשׁ
can also mean "in the sanctuary," thereby underlining the influence of the myth passages where the god is proclaimed supreme
in the council of the gods held in the sanctuary.

The texts of KTU 1.3 C 27, 64; 4 VII 49f can be compared to
vv 11a and 17b of the Song. But the text of v 11a can perhaps
better be compared to the myth of Marduk when he is proclaimed
supreme in the sanctuary after the defeat of Tiamat, Enuma
elish VI, 167; VII, 13.

VI 167: All of them uttering his name in the sanctuary
VII 13f: He is supreme in the assembly of the gods; no one
       among the gods is his equal.
Ex 15:11a: Who is like you among the gods, Yahweh, who is
       like you supreme in holiness (or in the sanctuary).

Because of the relationship to myth texts, and especially
because of the mention of the אֵלִם, the gods, some exegetes

have used this verse to establish an early dating for the Song[24]. But this cannot be done without first establishing when the form, meaning, and vocabulary of this verse were in use in Israelite life. Statements or questions about the incomparability of God in regard to the other gods are fairly common in the Old Testament, Ex 8:6 (P); 9:14 (J); 2 Sm 7:22 (D); 1 Kg 8:23 (D); Is 44:6-8; Jer 10:6f; 49:19; 50:44; Ps 18:32; 35:10; 86:8; 1 Chr 17:20; 2 Chr 6:14. Passages of incomparability where the other אֱלֹהִים are implied because God is the only true אֵל are found in Is 40:18; 43:10-12; 45:14, 21, 22; 46:9; 2 Sm 22:32; Dt 3:24 (the Deuteronomistic redactor); 33:26; Mic 7:18 (the redactor); Ps 77:14. Ps 89:6-9 is the only instance of an incomparability question where the אֱלֹהִים are explicitly mentioned.

It is probable that the form where the אֵל of Israel in contra-distinction to the other gods is the only really existent one begins in the exile. The concept appears in the latest Deuter-onomistic ambit and then heavily in Dt-Is. The only texts that can be argued for an earlier period are Dt 33:26 and 2 Sm 22:32. We have to elaborate upon them.

Dt 33:26 occurs within the context of the prophecies of Moses. All agree that the nuclear prophecies themselves are very ancient, but this text is part of the psalm that has been added to the prophecies and that frames them, Dt 33:1-5, 26-29. The phrase in question, אֵין כָּאֵל יְשֻׁרוּן, looks very much like a passage from the Song of Moses, Dt 32:12b, 15a. The Song of Moses is not specifically Deuteronomic, but it has been formulated so as to recall Deuteronomic themes which are especially prevalent in the late Deuteronomistic redactors[25]. Mayes places it in the exile because of the relation that it has to Dt-Is[26]. It is probable

---

24 Freedman, "Divine Names" 81.
25 Anthony Phillips, *Deuteronomy*, The Cambridge Bible Commentary (Cambridge, 1973) 209f, 215f.
26 Mayes, *Deuteronomy* 380ff.

that both the Song of Moses and the psalm framing the prophecies of Moses cannot be dated before the exile and that both come from poetic composers within the influence of the Deuteronomistic redactors and the school of Dt-Is.

The dating of the psalm of 2 Sm 22 is contested by exegetes, but the phrase in question looks exactly like the mentality of Dt-Is, especially when we include the variant in Ps 18:32:

2 Sm 22:32 מִי־ אֵל מִבַּלְעֲדֵי יהוה וּמִי צוּר מִבָּלְעֲדֵי אֱלֹהֵינוּ

Ps 18:32 מִי אֱלוֹהַּ

Is 44:6 וּמִבַּלְעָדַי אֵין אֱלֹהִים

Is 44:8b הֲיֵשׁ אֱלוֹהַּ מִבַּלְעָדַי וְאֵין צוּר בַּל ...

The mentality found in the Deuteronomistic redactors and Dt-Is is particularly fitting for the situation of the exile, when the Israelites were surrounded by peoples who worshipped other gods. The formulation is part of the exilic campaign that moves towards the more explicit statement of monotheism by the use of ever clearer formulations that the God of Israel is of a unique nature. Included in this campaign was the affirmation that no other אֵל was comparable to Yahweh. All of the statements treated above fit very well into this confrontational mentality. It is possible that all the instances of the incomparability of אֵל form are exilic or later. It is most clearly identified with the Deuteronomistic school and that of Dt-Is.

Whatever might be the case in regard to the origin of the general form of the incomparability of אֵל questions, Ps 77:14 and 89:6-9 show such an intense relation of vocabulary, form, and style to the specific formulation found in v 11a of the Song that they appear to all be from the same cultic ambit. Ps 77 and 89 use the incomparability of אֵל questions within the mentality of the current myth systems. They, like the Song, use the question to accompany highly mythical renditions of the conquest of the waters by God, 89:10f; 77:16-20. The vocabulary of each piece has a very strong correlation to both v 11a and 11b of the Song. Ps 89:6-9 can be compared to the entire vocabulary of Ex 15:11ab:

נוֹרָא פֶּלֶא	קֹדֶשׁ	בַּ	אֵלִם יהוה	בָּ	מִי־כָמֹכָה	Ex 15:11
פִּלְאֲךָ	בִּקְהַל קְדֹשִׁים					Ps 89:6
		בִּבְנֵי אֵלִים		מִי		Ps 89:7
בְּסוֹד־קְדֹשִׁים נוֹרָא						Ps 89:8
יהוה			מִי־כָמוֹךָ			Ps 89:9

Some exegetes have maintained that this passage is of an early date and have used the very strong similarity between it and the Song to maintain that the Song represents a period of early myth usage in Israel. This school insists that because there is so much similarity to Ugaritic myth forms present, this section of Ps 89 must be very early. The difficulty is that Ps 89 as a whole is certainly from sometime after the fall of the Davidic dynasty, because the whole sense of the psalm is the great disaster that has befallen the house of David despite the unconditional promise of God that it would go on forever. But the school which seeks to maintain the early dating of this myth passage contends that the psalm should be seen as a composite from different periods. Vv 6-19 would be a psalm that was composed very early[27].

But this theory cannot be sustained. The myth passage of the victory over the sea has the exact same stylistic form that is found in Ps 74:13-16, a psalm that is self evidently from the time after the destruction of the temple because 74:3-6 explicitly speaks about it. The two texts use the same technique of intro-

---

27 Ravasi 2:831; Cross, "Canaanite Myth" 135, 144.

ductory direct address to God to portray his action against the
waters. Each has a statement about a pair of opposites that
together comprise the whole of the system of creation belonging
to God, 74:16; 89:12, followed by a statement that God has put
a stable order in the universe. The myth descriptions themselves
portray the action whereby God has crushed the enemy waters,
which are also termed monsters. The two can be compared:

Ps 89:10-14		Ps 74:13-17	
אַתָּה 10b אַתָּה 10a		אַתָּה 13	
אַתָּה 11		אַתָּה 14	
		אַתָּה 15b אַתָּה 15a	
לְךָ שָׁמַיִם אַף־לְךָ אָרֶץ 12		לְךָ יוֹם אַף־לְךָ לָיְלָה 16a	
statement of stable 12b		statement of stable 16b	
order with אַתָּה		order with אַתָּה	
אַתָּה 13		אַתָּה 17b אַתָּה 17b	

Moreover, a similar form of direct address which introduces
the victory of Yahweh over the waters has been noted already
in Dt-Is, Is 51:9, 10, and all agree that the myth passage in Is
51 cannot be the interpolation of some earlier myth passage
into the text of Isaiah.

This direct address אַתָּה form is elsewhere present in the
acclamations to God the creator in the second temple liturgies.
It appears four times in Neh 9:6f, and three times in 2 Chr
20:6f.

To say that the myth rendering of Ps 89 is early while that of
Ps 74 is late, even though they both have the identical form,
both have a myth content that is indistinguishable in texture
and concept, both fall in contexts that demand that they can
only be read in the light of the events of the exile, and both use
a style that elsewhere is of exclusively late appearance, is not
reasonable. The conclusion of the school of poetry dating which

operates on the principle of similarity to Ugaritic poetry as its essential dating principle cannot be accepted.

In the placement of Ps 89 it must be noted that the entire interior dynamics of Ps 89 matches Ps 74. Ps 74 is a supplication that the temple be rebuilt. The recall of God's might at creation and the exodus is motive for trust that he can restore the temple. The myth section is integral to the supplication. Ps 74 has recourse to the election of Zion of old as part of the supplication that the temple be restored. The stability that God put into creation of old forms a base for his restoring the disorder that has come about by the fact that his temple has been destroyed.

In a similar way Ps 89 considers that the order of the universe is motive to hope for the restoration of the Davidic dynasty. God has established the heavens, v 12, and the throne of David will endure like the heavens, v 30. The stability of the Davidic dynasty has the same basis as that of the natural universe. See also vv 37, 38. Both the myth section of Ps 89 and the myth section of Ps 74 find themselves in the same context, the time when the pre-exilic institutions that had maintained Israelite life had been destroyed and not yet restored.

This way of reasoning where the order of Israelite institutions rests within God and the power by which he established order in the natural world pertains to the restoration period. Texts from the book of consolations of Jeremiah confirm this for they demonstrate the same type of reasoning that is found in Ps 89. The hope for the restoration of the ancient order in the new situation of the world of the return rests within the control that God has demonstrated over the waters and the general order that he has placed in the universe. In Jer 31:34-39 the hope for the general restoration of the people, 31:35b, 36b, and the rebuilding of the walls, 31:37-39, rest within God's control of nature, 31:35, 36a. In Jer 33:19-26 the hope for the restoration of the Davidic dynasty and the people in general also rests within the power that God has displayed in establishing regularity in nature. The following texts can then be compared:

שָׁמַיִם...מוֹסְדֵי־אֶרֶץ Jer 31:37a	שָׁמַיִם...אֶרֶץ...יְסַדְתָּם Ps 89:12
שֶׁמֶשׁ...יָרֵחַ Jer 31:35	כַשֶּׁמֶשׁ...כְּיָרֵחַ Ps 89:37b, 38
בְּרִיתִי...דָוִד Jer 33:21, 22	בְּרִית...לְדָוִד Ps 89:4f
עַבְדִּי	עַבְדִּי
כִּסְאוֹ...זֶרַע דָוִד עַבְדִּי	זַרְעֲךָ...כִּסְאֶךָ
וְדָוִד עַבְדִּי...מִזַּרְעוֹ Jer 33:26	לְדָוִד...זַרְעוֹ... Ps 89:36b, 37
	כִּסְאוֹ

In each of the texts the promises to David hinge on the regularity of nature. In Jer 33 it is the day and night, vv 20, 25, and the heaven and earth, v 25, that insure that Yahweh has not rejected the dynasty, and on which the hopes for its restoration are placed. In Ps 89 the firmness of the dynasty was built on the firmness of the heavens and earth, vv 3, 38, and is the cause for the lamentation at its downfall and the plea for its restoration. Ps 89 is certainly best placed in the time of the return, at some period when there were strong aspirations for the revival of the Davidic dynasty.

Ps 77:14 has an almost exact correlation to Ex 15:11a, while 77:15a has one of the specific formula phrases of Ex 15:11b,

מִי־כָמֹכָה בָּאֵלִם Ex 15:11a	מִי אֵל גָּדוֹל כֵּאלֹהִים Ps 77:14
(vocative) יהוה	(vocative) אֱלוֹהִים
בַּקֹּדֶשׁ...	בַּקֹּדֶשׁ
עֹשֵׂה פֶּלֶא Ex 15:11b	עֹשֵׂה פֶלֶא Ps 77:15a

יהוה is the identical to אֱלֹהִים when it is taken into account that Ps 77 is part of the Elohistic psalter.

The correlation between Ps 77 and the Song is more specific than that of Ps 89 because the myth passage that it follows has self consciously been applied to the exodus.

There are some who maintain that though Ps 77 is late, the myth passage is early because of its use of Ugaritic vocabulary[28], but this method has been shown above to be unacceptable. The interior evidence is very firm for placing the myth section with the rest of the psalm. The form of v 17 is a virtual repeat of v 2. And the exposition is the same as that which we saw in regard to a psalm of the same Asaphite school of the late period, Ps 74; the resolution to the present problem lies within the days of old, the days of God's control of the waters at the exodus.

Also, the myth language is very similar to Hab 3, which is an addition to the book and which most exegetes agree is of the same age or later[29]. Moreover, it has been demonstrated above that the myth section shows evidence of development from Dt-Isaian roots. So there is no valid reason to separate the myth section from the rest of this psalm.

Therefore, the use of these incomparability statements within the context of the myth mentality of the ancient near east appears in the late period. The two instances which are very close to the mentality of the Song are Ps 77 and 89. Ps 77 is of Asaphite origin, v 1. Ps 89 is of the school of Ethan, which in post-exilic times was counted among the Levites, and was very closely associated with the Asaphites, see 1 Chr 15:17, 19. Confirmation of the Levitical nature of the pertinent texts of Ps 89 can be gained from its close association with the redactive elements within the book of consolations of Jeremiah, which,

---

28 Ravasi 2:597ff.
29 Kaiser, *Einleitung* 244.

in turn, are of Levitical origin, see Jer 33:18, 21, and with the Levitical Ps 74 and 77.

In praise of God's great deeds, v 11b

All of the words found in this praise acclamation are of widespread use; still, an examination of the phrasing patterns here does reveal a clear ambit of style. The word נִפְלָאוֹת and the phrase עָשָׂה נִפְלָאוֹת are fairly common, and they are often used to portray the wonder of the exodus. But the specific phrase עָשָׂה פֶלֶא is restricted to the following texts: Is 25:1; Ps 77:15; 78:12; 88:11. All of these texts are post-exilic. Ps 77 and 78 are Asaphite. Ps 88 is of the school of Heman, which in the post-exile was of Levitical status and very closely associated with the Asaphites, 1 Chr 15:17, 19. Is 25:1 is of the redactive texts which virtually duplicated vv 1, 2, of the Song. It will be shown below that these redactive texts also can be described as being very close to the Asaphites (see p 183). Thus, the specific phrasing used is limited to the general Asaphite sphere.

Examination of this passage as a תְּהִלָּה phrase reveals the following: the conjunction of all of the four praise terms present in v 11b appears elsewhere only in Ps 106. In 106:12 the Israelites sing God's praises, but in v 13 they forget what he has just done. The thing that they have just forgotten is again spoken of in vv 21, 22. God is said to be a doer of great things, v 21b, but the great things are in parallelism with the wonders of v 22a. Thus the phrasing mentality of doer of wonders appears. Then both 21b and 22a are in parallelism with 22b, where it is proclaimed that God has done awesome things in Egypt.

A very similar phrasing mentality appears in Ps 78. In v 4 the Israelites are described as declaring the praises of Yahweh, which are styled the wonders that he did. In v 11 that action of the present generation is contrasted with their fathers who forgot the wonders that he did, vv 11f. Both Ps 106 and Ps 78 use the language in the same manner as the Song, to typify God's action at the Sea, Ps 106:7-11; 78:13. These two texts can be compared to the Song:

תְּהִלֹת Ex 15:11b	תְּהִלּוֹת Ps 78:4b	תְּהִלָּתוֹ Ps 106:12
נוֹרָא		נוֹרָאוֹת 22b
עָשָׂה פֶלֶא	עָשָׂה פֶלֶא 12	עָשָׂה...נִפְלָאוֹת 21a, 22b

These occurrences in Ps 78 and 106 are the only instances of תְּהִלָּה phrasing of this type in the scriptures, and they clearly conform to the specific type of confessional phrasing found in v 11b of the Song, the proclamation of what God did at the Reed Sea. The psalms are both of the post-exilic Asaphites.

The earth swallows up God's foes, v 12

V 12 takes up again the destruction of the Egyptians. The phrase תִּבְלָעֵמוֹ אָרֶץ is incongruous in a passage that purports to portray the destruction of the Egyptians in the sea, but fits quite well with the formulaic destruction language we found earlier. V 12 can be seen as continuing the thought of vv 4f and its closing acclamation lauding the right hand of Yahweh, v 6. Some of the late formulaic texts cited earlier in regard to vv 4f also demonstrate destruction in the earth as equivalent to destruction in the abyss, Ezk 26:19f; 31:15, 18; Jon 2:6f; Ps 71:20.

The specific word pair "the earth swallowed" appears elsewhere only in the descriptions of the incident of the rebellion in the desert, Nb 16:32, 34, 30 (J[30]); 26:10 (P); Dt 11:6; Ps 106:17.

---

30 Sources for Nb 16 are from Frederick L. Moriarty, "Numbers," *The Jerome Biblical Commentary* (Englewood Cliffs: Prentice Hall, 1968) 92.

The J story was about Abiram and Dathan who rebelled against Moses' authority. The Deuteronomistic redactors knew only this story, Dt 11:6. The story was expanded by P and reflects a controversy where there was an attempt by the Sons of Korah, a clan of gatekeepers and singers, to infringe upon the rights of the priests. This controversy had to take place in the second temple because P considers the Korahites to be Levites, Nb 16:7f, and they were not recognized as such until some time after the return[31]. It can be further specified that the controversy did not occur until after the reconstruction of the walls by Nehemiah, because the Korahite gatekeepers were not yet included among the Levites at the wall dedication ceremony, Neh 11:15-19. In the P redacted text of Nb 16 the eponymous ancestor of the Korahites becomes the main rebel, and Dathan and Abiram fall into second place. Eventually the dispute was resolved, see Nb 26:11.

Now the author of Ps 106 knows the P redacted text of Nb 16. The mention of the earth swallowing Dathan and Abiram, Ps 106:17, and the designation of the rebels as "the wicked," 106:18 are J, see Nb 16:26, 32. Aaron's description as the holy one, v 16, is central to P, Nb 16:3, 5, 7. Also, in v 17 the use to the term עֵדָה for the rebels is of the P redactor, Nb 16:3, 9, 11, 19, and the notion in v 18 that fire destroyed them is also P, Nb 16:35. But the author of Ps 106, though he mentions Dathan and Abiram, does not mention Korah. The obvious inference is that the reference to Korah was suppressed and that Ps 106 was written by someone with a friendly disposition toward the Korahites. This is confirmed in vv 30f of the psalm. It contains an eternal benediction of Phineas, and he was considered by the post-exilic singers to be the autochthonous patron of the Korahite clan, see 1 Chr 9:19f.

---

31 De Vaux, *Ancient Israel* 392f.

The above considerations fit well with the designation of Ps 106 as being of Asaphite authorship, a group of Levitical singers of the post-exile who were friendly towards the Korahites. The psalm then also dates from after the P redacted text of Nb 16, and can be placed at sometime after the reconstruction of the walls.

Some exegetes consider this psalm to be exilic[32]. The attribution is based on v 47. God is asked to save the Israelites from among the nations. But the prayer for a universal ingathering continues until the very end of the Old Testament period and into the New Testament, see Sir 36:10. The verse expressing the aspiration for the ingathering, Ps 106:47, follows directly upon v 46. The latter is a duplication of 1 Kg 8:50 which is demonstrably post-exilic, and which expresses concern for the diaspora[33].

If J. Watts is correct and both v 7bβ and 12b of the Song have been taken over from the rebellion in the desert[34], then the Song should be placed after the P addition to the Nb 16 text, because the notion of fire eating the rebels is limited to the P redaction. The source of the influence could be seen most clearly in a text like Nb 16:34, 35. V 34 is J, v 35 is P. That would place the Song well after the rebuilding of the walls by Nehemiah. But there is not sufficient reason to place vv 7bβ and 12b of the Song together. It can only be entertained as a possibility.

But if we consider v 12b alone, a case can be made for its having been influenced by the phrase as it appears in the rebellion story. The rebellion story belongs to the desert phase of Israelite history, especially as reported in confessional litera-

---

32 Roland E. Murphy, "Psalms," *The Jerome Biblical Commentary* (Englewood Cliffs: Prentice Hall, 1968) 595.

33 *The New Jerusalem Bible* note q to 1 Kg 8:41-51.

34 Watts, "Song" 272-274.

ture, Dt 11:6; Ps 106:17. V 12 of the Song appears in a position where the story of the defeat of the Egyptians has come to a close. So that its positioning brings to mind the desert phase and a takeover from the confessional literature's rendition of the rebellion, but for use according to its own purposes.

If v 12 of the Song is consciously using this phrase, then it is taking an anti-Korahite phrase and turning it away from them and from Israel as a whole and directing it towards the enemy. It would, therefore, be reflecting a similar attitude to that of Ps 106:16-18.

In the above treatment it is obvious that we are simply in the realm of speculation. That it somehow relates to the mentality of Ps 106 is simply a possibility. But what has more the texture of evidence is the fact that the use of the phrase in psalmic literature is restricted to the Asaphite Ps 106.

CHAPTER FIVE
EXEGESIS OF PART TWO, VV 13-17

The Leading Theme

Analysis of vv 13, 16b

In v 13 there starts a new theme, the arrival and entrance into the holy land. The leading and guiding passages of vv 13, 16b, although separated by the fear of the peoples interlude, should be treated as one piece. They portray the same notion of God's care for his people; עַם־זוּ גָּאָלְתָּ, "the people you have redeemed," is really the equivalent of עַם־זוּ קָנִיתָ, "the people you have purchased." The one phrase clearly continues the other because they both use the archaic expression זוּ. And both are the equivalent of 16ba עַמְּךָ," your people."

But these leading and guiding passages do not simply frame the fear of the peoples section, they interlock with it. The expression עַד־עָבַר, repeated in v 16b, is part of the fear of the peoples theme. The fear of the peoples extends from v 14-16b. V 16b, therefore, is a combination of both the leading theme and the fear of the peoples theme. In this section the leading theme will be treated. The phrase עַד־יַעֲבֹר will be treated along with the fear of the peoples theme in vv 14-16a.

The description is of God leading his people up to the holy land, v 13, and then into the holy land, v 16b. The overall tone of v 13 is pastoral. The depiction of God as pastor does not rest on the verb נָחָה, for the term only has the general sense of to lead and does not of itself have a necessarily pastoral implications[1]. נהל means to lead to a watering station and cause to rest there[2]. It often has pastoral connotations, but not exclusively. נָוֶה, though, must place the text within the pastoral ambit. It has the specific meaning of the abode of a shepherd or the flocks[3].

This mode of description, God leading his people as a pastor at the exodus, is not part of the original exodus leading and guiding tradition. The J and E traditions have God leading the people, but never as pastor, Ex 13:17 (E), 21 (J[4]), and the convention remains constant into the post-exile, see Ps 78:14, Neh 9:12, 19. This tradition is distinct from the representation of God leading or caring for his people as pastor at the exodus. The two can be seen existing simultaneously in Ps 78. V 14 is the tradition based within the early exodus depiction; vv 52f are the depiction of God leading as pastor. Each has its own form.

The overall notion of God the pastor leading his people out of slavery into their land is something that only appears with the exile, and is first applied to the return. The theme is found in the exilic and post-exilic schools of the prophets. Is 40:11; 49:10; Ezk 34:13-16 are depictions of the return; in Mic 7:14f[5] the author is also speaking of the return but with explicit mention of the exodus. The theme is applied to the God of the exodus only in the post-exile, Ps 74:1b 2; 77:21; 78:52f; Is 63:11-14. The psalmic instances are limited to the Asaphite school.

---

1 Francis Brown, S. R. Driver, and Charles A. Briggs, eds., *A Hebrew and English Lexicon of the Old Testament* (Oxford, 1951) 634f.
2 Brown, Driver, and Briggs 624f.
3 Brown, Driver, and Briggs 627.
4 Hyatt, *Exodus* 148.
5 Mays 155-169.

An examination of the vocabulary and its use found in vv
13, 16b will verify in a rigorous fashion that all of the notions
portrayed have their origin in the exilic and post-exilic schools
of the prophets and that the specific usages show the marks of
the development of those notions as carried out in the post-exilic
school of the Asaphites.

We have noted that the term נהג is not of itself pastoral, but
when by its context it is verified as a description of Yahweh
pastor of Israel, it is limited to Asaphite psalm, Ps 77:21; 78:53.
In Ps 77:21 the pastoral sense is clear because God is said to
have lead his people like a flock. In Ps 78:53 the people God
leads are the same ones he leads like a flock of sheep in v 52.
In both instances it refers to the action of God in the exodus:
77:21 speaks of the ministration of Moses; 78:53 speaks of the
destruction of the Egyptians at the Sea.

The word used to describe God's action of redemption of the
people from Egypt by the act of the exodus in v 13 of the Song
is גאל, a term of legal origin. The גּוֹאֵל is a near relation who
protects the rights of the members of the clan. He avenges any
death to a member of the clan, Dt 19:6, 12; Js 20:5, 9, etc. He
also buys back any land that has been sold outside the clan or
is about to be sold, Jer 32:7-9; Ru 4:1-10; Lv 25:25-34; 27:13-34.
He can also buy back a clan member who has been sold into
slavery, 25:47-55.

The term is applied to God as the one who protects the
individual in danger, Gn 48:16; Prov 23:11; Ps 19:15; 69:19,
etc. It can also be applied to Yahweh as protector of Israel as a
whole, something which occurs 34 times. One of these is pre-
exilic, Hos 13:14, but it should be noted that although the idea
that Yahweh can be redeemer of Israel is entertained, he refuses.
Texts where Yahweh acts as redeemer of Israel are always exilic
and post-exilic. The notion appears at its earliest in texts that

are Dt-Isaian, Is 41:14; 43:1, 14; 44:6, 22, 23, 24; 47:4; 48:17, 20; 49:7, 26; 51:10; 52:3, 9; 54:5, 8, or texts influenced by Dt-Isaian thought, Is 35:9; 59:20; 60:16; 62:12; 63:9, 16; Jer 31:11; 50:34; Mic 4:10 (the redactor[6]); Ex 6:6 (P[7]); Ps 74:2; 77:16; 78:35; 106:10; 107:2 bis. It can be noted that all of the psalmic instances are Asaphite, except for Ps 107, which is of the second temple Levites.

The idea was originally applied to the redemption from exile because גאל has the sense of to buy back, to redeem from something. The idea does not well apply to the initial act of forming the people, because it has the idea of buying back what has already been owned. The formation of the people would have the sense of an initial purchase.

The application of the term to the exodus takes place at its earliest, again, in Dt-Is. Its employment for the exodus comes about by the transfer of the notion from the return to the exodus, because the return was seen by Dt-Is as a new exodus. What was predicated of the new exodus would then have to be applicable to the original exodus. Thus, in 48:20f גאל is mentioned in a passage that implicitly speaks about the return through the desert as a new exodus where there will be a new pouring of water from the rock. Explicit use of גאל to describe the exodus then occurs in Is 51:10; 63:9, 16; Ps 74:2; 77:16; 78:35; 106:10. All of the psalmic instances are Asaphite. The development is our oft repeated scheme: from the school of Deutero-Isaiah to the school of the Asaphites.

Also with the term קנה, v 16b, there is a similar outline that presents itself. When the term is used to denote God's purchase of Israel, it is always late. In Is 11:11 it means the restoration

---

6 John Smith, *Micah, Zephaniah and Nahum*, The International Critical Commentary (Edinburgh: T and T Clark, 1912) 97.
7 Hyatt, *Exodus* 93.

and universal ingathering, but as a redoing of the exodus, 11:16. In the other texts it explicitly refers to the exodus, Dt 32:6; Ps 74:2; 78:54. The psalmic instances are of the school of Asaph.

It can be objected that the text of Ps 78:54 refers to the Israelite territory, the mountain that God purchased, and does not refer to the people. But in the Asaphite mind the territory, the tribes, and the people are not totally distinct. See 74:2, where the congregation, the tribe, and the mountain appear in parallelism.

The whole rest of the formulation of these verses brings us very clearly within the same ambit. The phrase עַם־זוּ, vv 13, 16b, appears elsewhere only in Is 43:21. There the phrase is עַם־זוּ יָצַרְתִּי, "the people I formed." It has a reference to the initial formation of the people at the exodus, see 43:15-17; and in Dt-Isaian thought this is really equivalent to the Song phrase עַם־זוּ גָּאָלְתִּי; see 43:1; 44:24, where יָצַר and גָּאַל are in parallelism.

נָהַל, v 13, is applied to God leading his people only by Dt-Is, 40:11; 49:10; 51:18[8].

God is said to lead his people to his נָוֶה. The use of this term as the place where God demonstrates his care for his people is always late, from the exile or post-exile. It is appears as the place where God brings his people in Jer 23:3; 31:23; 33:12; 50:19; Ezk 34:14, or where his people have repose in Is 32:18; 33:20; 65:10. It is always speaking of the return[9].

---

8   It appears in 2 Chr 32:22, but the reading is rejected by the critics. See Elliger note b to 2 Chr 32:22; *The New Jerusalem Bible* note b to 2 Chr 32:22.

9   Hos 9:13 speaks of the Israelites being planted in a meadow, and this is in the general context of the entrance from the wilderness, 9:10. But it is not probable that we have the original text here. All critics consider the text corrupt and most follow the Greek. See Elliger note b to Hos 9:13.

The specific phrase נְוֵה קֹדֶשׁ appears only once elsewhere, in parallelism, Jer 31:23. The book of the consolations of Jeremiah has been shown above to evidence the hands of Levitical redactors. It can be shown with considerable certainty that this phrase can be attributed to them, and more precisely, to the hands of the Levitical cult singers of the second temple. The phrasing depicting the return in 31:23 can be compared to 33:10-12:

			בְּשׁוּבִי אֶת־שְׁבוּתָם	31:23
			אָשִׁיב אֶת־שְׁבוּת	33:11
נְוֵה	יֹאמְרוּ ...	עוֹד	כֹּה־אָמַר יהוה צְבָאוֹת ...	31:23
אֹמְרִים		עוֹד ...	כֹּה־אָמַר יהוה	33:10
אֹמְרִים				11
		יהוה צְבָאוֹת	אֶת	
נְוֵה		עוֹד ...	כֹּה־אָמַר יהוה צְבָאוֹת	12

We are within the same redactional sphere in both of these passages. And 33:10-12 is of the hand of the Levitical singers of the second temple because 33:11a is their refrain. It will be shown below that this refrain belongs most especially to the clan of the Asaphites, who were the dominant group of singers in the post-exile (see below p 182).

Confirmation that this line comes from within the Levitical singers and from the sphere of the Asaphites can be found in the psalmic verse found in 31:25. This is a duplicate of the style of a verse from a psalm of the Levitical singers, Ps 107:9. So that there is extensive evidence that the Levitical clans have placed Jer 31:23-25 as an interpolation here.

Further verification that we are within general range of the Asaphite school can be gained from the following: the only instance of the use of נְוֵה in the book of Psalms, in any context, is Ps 79:7, an Asaphite psalm. Moreover, the Asaphites have shown themselves to have interjected their נָוֶה phrasing in the book of Jeremiah. The exact phrase appears in a post-exilic psalmic addition to the book, Jer 10:25. It is a good presumption that the נָוֶה phrase of Jer 31:22 is also an interjection of the school of Asaph or someone close to it. Thus the phrase נָוֶה קָדְשֶׁךָ in v 13b of the Song shows ties that converge on the Asaphite phrasing mentality.

The Structure of vv 13-17

The people of Yahweh are the dominant theme in vv 13, 16b. Commentators have frequently noted that there is no mention of the Israelites in the first part of the Song, which tells of the mythical action of God on the waters and the destruction of the Egyptians. The Israelites are inferred because in v 9 the Egyptians plan to pursue someone into the standing water. That statement is incomprehensible unless the previous entrance of the Israelites is presumed. Still, there is no explicit mention of the Israelites until v 13. There they are described as the people, עַם, that Yahweh has obtained and whom he leads.

This juxtaposition of Reed Sea myth text or destruction of the Egyptians text, which has no mention of the Israelites, and pastoral leading texts in which God leads his people, is Asaphite in nature. It is most clearly seen in Ps 77:16-21. The myth rendition, vv 17-20, does not mention the Israelites; its only theme is the conflict of God and the water, but it is juxtaposed with pastoral leading expressions where God is pastor and Israel is the flock, vv 16, 21.

Moreover, 77:16, 21 show the exact thought form found in v 13 of the Song, and the vocabulary matches up.

Ex 15:13   נָחִיתָ ... עַם־זוּ   גָּאָלְתָּ ... בְּעָזְּךָ

Ps 77:21   נָחִיתָ ...

עַמֶּךָ

Ps 77:16   גָּאַלְתָּ ...

עַמֶּךָ

Ps 77:15b   עֻזֶּךָ

It can be further stated that additional structural mentality running from v 13 to v 16 of the Song is duplicated in Ps 77:16-21. Both of the texts have two lines that, though they are separated by an intervening interlude, interlock, with the notion of "your people" being the link held in common. The intervening interludes also have almost identical styles. The fear text of Ps 77:17-20 concerns the fear of the waters, whereas the fear of the peoples is spoken of in the Ex 14-16a. But the initiating fear description is similar with the use of רגז and חול. And the same acclamatory style is found in Ps 77:17a and Ex 15:16b. The forms are exact duplicates: a/b/יהוה; a/b/c. Ps 77:17a has אֱלֹהִים, but that is attributable to the fact that it is in the Elohistic psalter. The overall structural equivalence of Ps 77:16-21 and vv 13-16b of the Song is remarkable:

Ex 15:13a   עַם זוּ   Ps 77:16a   עַמֶּךָ

Fear Interlude 14-16b   Fear Interlude 17-20

14   יִרְגָּזוּן ... חִיל   17   יָחִילוּ ... יִרְגְּזוּ

a/b/יהוה (voc); a/b/c 16b   a/b/אֱלֹהִים (voc); a/b/c 17a

Ex 15:16b   עַם זוּ ... עַמְּךָ   Ps 77:21   עַמֶּךָ

The two pieces have virtually the same structural mentality, one which cannot be accounted for by imitation; the correspondences are far too pervasive and subtle for that. These two texts must be from the same psalmic school.

Ps 77, therefore, has a structural mentality that extends through much of part two of the Song, and which also accounts for the motifs that dominate each part of the Song, the water text and the pastoral leading text. Moreover, the formulas that accompany the water myth texts of part one of the Song, v 11ab, were seen to be present in Ps 77:14, 15a (pp 119f). Ps 77 must be of the same stylistic school of psalmic composers who are responsible for our text.

Something similar can be seen in Ps 74:12-17. It also has no mention of the Israelites. Only God's mythical defeat of the waters is spoken of. The juxtaposition of this event with the notion of Yahweh pastor of the flock is also present. The events are described as what God did of old, קֶדֶם, v 12a. This interlocks with the people Yahweh obtained of old, v 2. These people are the sheep of whom Yahweh is the pastor, v 1.

This portrayal of the people of God corresponds to the whole flow of the action in part two of the Song. The description of these people as those that God redeemed and bought in, 74:2, can be compared to vv 13 and 16b of the Song. The tribe of God's inheritance is identified with mount Zion and is also the same as the sanctuary of 74:7. Compare all of the Song's leading theme, including the sanctuary entrance in v 17, to Ps 74:

Ex 15:13, 16b עַמְּךָ קָנִיתָ, גָּאַלְתָּ	עֲדָתְךָ קָנִיתָ, גָּאַלְתָּ Ps 74:2
17 הַר נַחֲלָתְךָ	2 נַחֲלָתֶךָ הַר
מִקְדַשׁ אֲדֹנָי	7 מִקְדָּשֶׁךָ

The same juxtaposition of themes can be found in the second mention of the Reed Sea event in Ps 78, vv 52-54. Here the destruction of the Egyptians, v 53b, is bracketed by expressions of God leading his people pastorally to his sacred area. Vv 52, 53a, 54a have a perfect equivalence to v 13 of the Song.

The description of the entrance into the land in Ps 78 has the same dynamics that are found in the Song. The people first come to the border of the land, which as a whole is considered sacred, v 54. That land is termed a mountain that they inherit, vv 54b, 55a. But the true term of the movement is the mountain of Zion on which is the sanctuary that God has built, vv 68f. That progression of events is very similar to what is found in the Song. In v 13 the people come to the border of the land which as a whole is considered sacred, they enter in and come to the mountain of God's inheritance, which is the same as his sanctuary that he has built himself, v 17.

The extreme similarity of vocabulary and concept can be seen by comparing the two texts:

נָחִיתָ, עַם Ex 15:13 Ps	עַמּוֹ, יַנְחֵם 78:52
אֶל־נְוֵה קָדְשֶׁךָ	אֶל־גְּבוּל קָדְשׁוֹ 54a
קָנִיתָ 16b	קָנְתָה 54b
תְּבִאֵמוֹ ... בְּהַר נַחֲלָתְךָ 17	יְבִיאֵם ... הַר ... נַחֲלָה ... 54, 55a
הַר ... מִקְּדַשׁ אֲדֹנָי	הַר צִיּוֹן ... מִקְדָּשׁוֹ 68, 69
God's sanctuary which he has built	God's sanctuary which he has built

It is eminently clear that all of the structural thinking found in common in the Song and Ps 74, 77, 78 has to come from within the Asaphite school. None of it can be called an imitation of or a patterning after the Song of the Sea. It is far to diffuse and ingrained into the works. It is a mentality of the school of psalmic writers that is present in all of the works.

Also, none of the major themes involved in this structural network has been brought into these Asaphite psalms from outside. They are of favored treatment in their own works. It has already been discussed that the treatment of the Reed Sea event is of frequent occurrence in their school, Ps 74, 77, 78, 106. The notion of pastoral care and leading of the people of Israel in general is a preferred theme of the Asaphites, Ps 74:1f; 77:21; 78:52, 71f; 79:13; 80:2. God's inheritance is also of the Asaphite mind and appears everywhere, 74:2; 78:55, 62, 71; 79:1; 82:8. מִקְדָּשׁ is also an almost exclusive usage of their school; all but one instance in psalmic literature, 68:36, appear within their corpus, 73:17; 74:7; 78:69; 96:6.

Thus the whole of the structural similarities which reproduce the second part of the Song in Ps 74, 77, 78 are of Asaphite origin and have been generated from within the school. Also the relation of themes of parts one and two of the Song is of Asaphite conception.

The Liturgical Character of vv 13, 16b, 17

Vv 13, 16b, 17 on the historical level tell of the entrance of the people into the Holy Land, but it can be demonstrated that on the cultic level they represent entrance into the temple in Jerusalem.

The people are represented as arriving at God's נוה קדשׁ, holy dwelling. The term appears one other place in Scripture, in parallelism, Jer 31:23. From the layout of the Jeremian passage the whole land is indicated because it speaks of all of Judah dwelling on the holy mountain. But the commentators are also agreed that the author has Jerusalem and the temple in mind as well[10]. It has been shown above that the expression found in Jer 31:23 is very likely from the same school of thought as that found in the Song of the Sea. In fact the Song also

---

10 Carroll 605-607; James Philip Hyatt, "The Book of Jeremiah," *The Interpreter's Bible*, vol. 5 (Nashville: Abingdon, 1956) 1034f.

indicates by the positioning of the phrase at the moment of arrival that the whole land is being referred to, but the use of קֹדֶשׁ would already place the reader into a cult and temple mentality. The land as a whole is seen as centered in the sanctuary.

This can be confirmed by an examination of Ps 78:54. It has already been shown that in this line we have an exact conceptual duplicate of the arrival at the holy land portrayed in v 13 of the Song. In Ps 78:54 the people arrive at the holy border, obviously the boundary of the Holy Land, because the following verses speak about the expulsion of the natives. But even though the verse is speaking about the land as a whole, the real term of the entrance progression is Mt Zion, v 68, and the sanctuary that Yahweh will build on it, v 69. Such is also the progression of the Song where the people arrive ultimately at the sanctuary that God has built, v 17b.

Moreover, it can be confirmed that the author of Ps 78 is already thinking of the land as the place of the temple. V 54b, which is the description of the land, and v 68, the description of the temple site, can both be compared with another Asaphite psalm, 74:2:

78:54b, 68 הַר־זֶה קָנְתָה, הַר צִיּוֹן   74:2 קָנִיתָ, הַר־צִיּוֹן זֶה

Both texts then make the mountain equivalent to the מִקְדָּשׁ, which is Jerusalem and the temple on it, Ps 74:7; 78:69. The usages held in common by Ps 74 and 78 are exact enough to state that these verses are certainly from the same school of thinking and probably from the same hand. The same mode of description that is used for the land as a whole in 78:54 is used to describe the temple site in 74:2. The land is centered in Zion and the temple. Now the same mode of thinking that we have in Ps 78:54 can reasonably be attributed to the Song because, as was shown above, Ps 78 also represents the mind of the Song.

The people cross over, Ex 15:16b, and proceed further, entering into and being established in the mountain that God has inherited, v 17a. This phrase only appears in one other place, again in parallelism, in the Asaphite Ps 74:2ab. The term שֵׁבֶט, tribe, almost certainly means the tribal land as well as the tribes themselves, see 78:68. But the final referent is to Zion and the temple, vv 3-6. Thus it also has a concentric quality; the land takes on its meaning from the temple within it.

מָכוֹן לְשִׁבְתְּךָ, place of your dwelling, appears elsewhere as the exact phrase, that is, with the particle לְ, only in 1 Kg 8:13 and its parallel 2 Chr 6:2. It is used to describe the temple in the original dedication ceremony.

מִקְדָשׁ אֲדֹנָי, sanctuary of the Lord, elsewhere is found only in Lam 2:20, where the exact phrase occurs. This phrase is not a quote; rather it is a development from within its own usages. This is evident because it is a restatement of the same terms that are found in 2:7 in parallelism. In both instances it means the temple.

All of the phrases used of the place of arrival in all of their appearances in Scripture have Jerusalem as their final referent. In two of these appearances we are in contact with what is very likely the same school of thought that has written the Song of the Sea. Thus it can be concluded that the Song of the Sea is speaking of entrance into the temple in Jerusalem.

The temple cult nature of vv 13, 17 is confirmed in that their overall formulation corresponds very closely to formulas for the entrance of the individual into the temple. This can be shown by comparing these verses to Ps 43:3f. In Ps 43:3 there are the consecutive terms of bringing in by God with the repetition of the suffix, that are also found in v 17a of the Song. In addition, there is the notion of entering the mountain which is at the same time the sacred place.

Also, the supplicant seeks that God will send guides to accompany him. These are quasi-personified attributes of the deity. One of these is God's truth, 43:3, the other is God's חֶסֶד, 42:9. This mode of being brought into the sanctuary is the conceptual duplicate of the Song where God's חֶסֶד and his strength act as guides for the entering people, v 13.

The whole scenario can be seen more clearly in Ps 5:8f, also a description of temple entrance of the individual worshipper. The worshipper enters, בּוֹא, by the חֶסֶד of God into the sacred temple, הֵיכַל־קָדְשְׁךָ, v 8, and he is lead, נחה, by the righteousness of God, v 9. The repetition of the attributes of God in the form of בְּ...ךְ can be compared to v 13 of the Song.

The point to be gained here is that the Song has the same form as that of a temple entrance. The בּוֹא of v 17a is both a description of the historical entrance into the Holy Land and the בּוֹא of cult entrance.

The notion that God brought the Israelites into the Holy Land is one of the fundamental articles of the faith and appears in the earliest layers of tradition, especially with בּוֹא in the *hiph'îl*, as is found in v 17a. And this expression is especially prominent in Dt, see 4:38; 6:10; 7:1 etc. But the notion that the entrance into the Holy Land is coterminous with entrance into Mt. Zion and the temple is foreign to all early traditions. If Ex 23:20 means to indicate the temple, which I believe is likely, then it has its first appearance in the Deuteronomistic redactors[11]. In texts with explicit mention of the temple it does not

---

11 For temple motifs here see p142 below. That it is Deuteronomic is commonly held. Childs, *Exodus* 486, holds that the passage is a late homily from an unspecified date, which uses pre-Deuteronomic material, such as the motif of the guiding angel. Hyatt, *Exodus* 250f, has proven that it is either contemporary to or post-dates the latest layers of the

appear before the exilic prophets and regards the return, Is 27:13; 35:10; 51:11; 56:7f; Jer 31:10; Ezk 40:1-3 (in vision); Neh 1:9; Ps 43:3, always with the double use of בֹּוא, as entrance into the holy land and as temple entrance. Its application to the exodus and initial entrance as cultic is found in explicit form only in the Asaphite Ps 78:54. The usage in Ps 78:54 gives indication that it has taken the Isaian notion for the return and applied it to the exodus:

Ps 78:54   וַיְבִיאֵם   אֶל־גְּבוּל קָדְשֹׁו
הַר ...

Is 56:7   וַהֲבִיאֹותִים אֶל־הַר   קָדְשִׁי

Thus, the development of the notion follows a pattern that we have seen repeatedly: a first appearance in Dt-Is, then a takeover of the usage by the Asaphites to reach the conceptual status that it has in the Song of the Sea.

Once this double character of the text has been established, the following can be said: the notion that the whole land is holy, or its corollary, that the whole land is a sanctuary, v 13b, never appears until the post-exile. It is stated in the already mentioned Jer 31:23 and Ps 78:54, then elsewhere only in Ps 114:2.

נטע, v 17a, to plant, when it is used figuratively to describe the care of God for Israel, appears in one text which is probably early, Nb 24:6, then in the Deuteronomistic redactor, 2 Sm 7:10. But when it is used to describe God bringing Israel into the land, it is always late. It describes the return in Jer 24:6; 32:41; Ezk 36:36. It portrays the initial entrance in Ps 44:3; 80:9, 16. The Asaphite Ps 80 has an extensive development of the theme.

Deuteronomistic redactors and thoroughly Deuteronomistic in tenor.

Inheritance, נַחַל, v 17, is one of the primary legal terms in Israel, and is often used in regards to land ownership. But the notion that the land is God's inheritance is only late, appearing in Jer 2:7; 16:18; 50:11, and perhaps 12:7-9. When it refers to the temple and Jerusalem it only occurs in the post-exile. Zech 2:16 portrays the theme of God inheriting the land of Judah, but places it in parallelism with Jerusalem. The simple statement of the city and temple being the inheritance of Yahweh are found only in the Asaphite corpus, Ps 74:2; 79:1.

מָכוֹן means a fixed place. It is found with some frequency with reference to the heavenly place where God dwells, 1 Kg 8:39, 43, 49; Is 18:4. But the term is never applied to Jerusalem and its temple except in post-exilic texts, 1 Kg 8:13; 2 Chr 6:2; Ezr 2:68; Is 4:5[12]; Dn 8:11. (For the discussion on 1 Kg 8:13 see below pp 144-146).

יָשַׁב, literally to sit, but also in the sense of to dwell, is predicated of God from early times, Ps 29:10; 1 Kg 8:30, 39; 22:19; Is 6:1 bis; Sm 4:4, etc. But it is never predicated of God's residing in Jerusalem until the post-exile, Ps 9:12; 68:17; 132:13f; 1 Kg 8:13; 2 Chr 6:2.

מִקְדָּשׁ literally indicates an open air sanctuary, not a building. In its proper use it appears from early times, Am 7:9, 13; Is 16:12; Js 24:26. As referring to the Jerusalem temple it occurs 52 times, always in the exilic and post-exilic periods: Is 60:13; 63:18; Jer 17:12 (an addition); 51:51; Lam 1:10; 2:7, 20; Ezk 5:11; 8:6; 9:6; 21:7; 23:38, 39; 24:21; 25:3; 28:18; 37:26, 28; 43:21; 44:1, 5, 7, 8, 9, 11, 15, 16; 45:3, 4, 4, 4, 18; 47:12; 48:8, 10, 21; Dn 8:11; 9:17; 11:31; Ps 68:36; 73:17; 74:7; 78:69; 96:6; Neh 10:40; 1 Chr 22:19; 28:10; 2 Chr 20:8; 26:18; 29:21; 30:8; 36:17.

---

12 From the Persian period according to Kaiser, *Isaiah 1-12* 85.

The term has its first appearance in this sense in Ezk, and is a prominent usage there occurring twenty-nine times. He has no doubt taken it over from the P circle where it is a favorite term. It is used fourteen times to describe the desert tent shrine, but always with the temple of Jerusalem in mind. See the Code of Holiness, Lv 19:30; 20:3; 21:12, 12, 23; 26:2, 31, and the P author, Ex 25:8; Lv 12:4; 16:33; Nb 3:38; 10:21; 18:1; 19:20.

The term appears five times in psalmic literature, and as already noted four of them are Asaphite, Ps 73:17; 74:7; 78:69; 96:6. The only exception is Ps 68:36, which is part of the adaptation of the psalm to the liturgy of the second temple.

The verb כון, to establish, appears in a passage where God establishes the land as a whole in Ex 23:20. But this is a late Deuteronomistic passage so the temple cannot be far from his mind when he speaks of the place which he has established. Note the basic Deuteronomistic temple language present in Ex 23:20f: "my name is in him," and מָקוֹם for place, which can be compared to the description of the temple in 1 Kg 8:6f, 21. Whether we believe this is a in some way a temple text or not, it does point up the Deuteronomistic roots of this usage, for this is the earliest text of this type. Then כון as explicitly predicated of the temple and Jerusalem is only post-Deuteronomic, Is 2:2; 62:7; Jer 33:2; Ps 48:9; 87:5; 107:36, probably all post-exilic[13]. The psalmic instances are of one or another of the clans of temple singers.

The general conclusion is that the entrance verses speak on a surface level about the first entrance of the people into the land as a whole, but all the language, phrasing, and usage indicates a post-exilic temple entrance psalm.

---

13 In regard to Is 2 see Kaiser, *Isaiah 1-12* 25; Gray 42ff, Lindblom 384 note 182, 283. There is general consensus regarding Ps 87; see Ravasi 2:792. For Ps 48 see pp 170-174 below.

V 17 as Myth Text

The mythical nature of v 17 has rightly been pointed out. מָכוֹן לְשִׁבְתְּךָ, the place for your sitting, is certainly related to the place where all the gods sit upon their thrones in the assembly of the gods. It is found in the Marduk story, Enuma elish IV, 1f, 11-14; VI, 74; VII, 10.

Attention has been drawn, especially by Cross, to the congruence of language between mountain of your inheritance, v 17a, and the Baal myth language for the sanctuary of the god[14], see KTU 1.3 C, 27; D, IV, 64. The use of sitting to describe the place where the gods dwell is very prominent in Ugaritic myth also, and the root יָשַׁב is the one commonly employed, 1.3 E, 3-6; E, V, 46-52; 1.4, I, 10-19. But the influence of Ugaritic myth is more clearly in evidence if we examine the other place where the phrase occurs, 1 Kg 8:13. There the term יָשַׁב is placed in apposition with זְבֻל, lofty. This word pair is also standard for describing the palace that is built for the god, see KTU 1.2, III, 8, 19f; 2, I 21, 24; 2, IV, 7.

This evidence of Ugaritic influence has played a large part in the system of Cross and Freedman for dating the Song of the Sea as very ancient. But while the evidence for Ugaritic influence is valid, the time period when this influence was felt has not been established.

We have already seen that in the Scripture נחל is not predicated of God until late, and not used for God's sanctuary until the post-exile. The use in Ps 74:2 is specifically mythical and of the mentality of the Song, but it is clearly of post-exilic provenience. Thus the use of this myth concept is indicative of late dating.

---

14 Cross, "Canaanite Myth" 125.

The instance outside the Song of מָכוֹן לְשִׁבְתְּךָ, 1 Kg 8:13, has to be examined in detail. All have rightly seen that the verse stands outside the rest of the formulation of the temple dedication text. It is mythopoetic in nature and has no contact with the source material or the Deuteronomistic redactor. Commentators uniformly then place it as very early poetry that perhaps touches the dedication ceremony of Solomon itself[15]. But the fact that it is outside the other material and is mythopoetic does not relegate it to ancient status. It must be further proven when it came to be written.

The pronouncement of 1 Kg 8:13 is an affirmation that Solomon has built a house for Yahweh's dwelling. But if we go back to the most ancient tradition we find that the notion of a place of dwelling cannot be applied to Yahweh. In 2 Sm 7:5, 6, which most commentators agree is of an early level of the text[16]. God asks a question about whether David can build a house for his dwelling, הַאַתָּה תִּבְנֶה־לִּי בַיִת לְשִׁבְתִּי. And the presumed answer is an emphatic "no." This is in direct contradiction to the affirmation about Yahweh's dwelling in 1 Kg 8:13, בָּנֹה בָנִיתִי בֵּית ... לְשִׁבְתֶּךָ . And this is an emphatic affirmation because of the presence of the infinitive.

It is not that early tradition is ignorant of the general usages found in the myth of Baal building his temple. It shows that the Canaanite notions had certainly entered Israel. Besides the Ugaritic יֹשׁב texts already mentioned, compare the building phrase of 2 Sm 7:5b with KTU 1.4, V, 26f, and the house of cedars of 7:7b with 1.4, V 9. Besides, when Israel did construct the temple, it did so in heavy dependence on the king of Tyre, David's lifelong friend, 1 Kg 5:15-20, whose basic presuppositions

---

15 Simon J. De Vries, *1 Kings*, Word Biblical Commentary 12 (Waco: Word Books, 1985) 122.

16 P. Kyle McCarter, *II Samuel*, The Anchor Bible (Garden City: Doubleday, 1984) 223. 2 Sam 7:5b-7 is early, though not of the first layer.

would be Baalistic. The Baalistic myth elements are clearly present, and it is exactly those elements that are rejected.

The reason for the rejection is that they portray a fixed and unchangeable residence for the deity. In early Israelite tradition that kind of residence can never be predicated of Yahweh in regard to any earthly place. Yahweh can be described as sitting or dwelling above the heavenly cherubim, represented by the figures on the Ark, 1 Sm 4:4; 2 Sm 6:2; 2 Kg 19:15, or the ark can be spoken of as dwelling in a place, 1 Sm 7:2; 2 Sm 6:11, but the ark itself has the sense of portability, 2 Sm 7:2. However, the term יָשַׁב is denied of any building, which would naturally be bound to a place[17].

The tradition present in 1 Sm 7:6 is that Yahweh can be in a tent or a מִשְׁכָּן, a portable shrine. There is no evidence that the notion that Yahweh cannot reside in any fixed place changed between the time of David and the time of the Deuteronomistic historians. Even when the temple is built and Yahweh's presence is transferred from tent to permanently constructed building, the mode of Yahweh's presence must be carefully adapted so as not to infringe on the principle of his own portability. The solution of the Deuteronomistic school is that Solomon will build a temple to the "name of Yahweh," 2 Sm 7:13; 1 Kg 8:18, 20, 44; 9:3.

Then there is a careful distinction in the use of יָשַׁב in regard to Yahweh. The verb is affirmed of Yahweh's residence in heaven consistently, 1 Kg 8:30, 39, 43, 49; 22:19; Is 6:1. But it is denied to Yahweh's manner of residence on earth. The same type of question expecting an emphatic "no" that we saw in 2 Sm 7:5 reappears in 1 Kg 8:27. "Can God really dwell on the earth? Behold, the heavens and the highest heavens cannot

---

17 A. A. Anderson, *2 Samuel*, Word Biblical Commentary 11 (Waco: Word Books, 1989) 120.

contain him, how much the less this house which I have built?"
Here it is denied that Yahweh can dwell anywhere on earth.
Also compare the careful distinction between מָקוֹם used alone
for the temple, 8:29, and מָקוֹם שִׁבְתְּךָ used of Yahweh's proper
residence in heaven, 8:30. The Deuteronomistic tradition of
temple building is very clear to reserve יָשַׁב for use only of
Yahweh's abode in heaven. Nor is there any pre-exilic text that
can be found to predicate it of his residence on earth. It is part
of the continuing temple construction tradition that you cannot
speak of Yahweh as dwelling in a permanent manner in a fixed
place; it would limit him.

The same is true regarding מָכוֹן. It has a sense of utter
fixity, permanence. As late as the Deuteronomistic period It is
used for Yahweh's residence in heaven, 1 Kg 8:39, 43, 49, But
never applied to his residence on the earth.

But the same terms, יָשַׁב and מָכוֹן, are affirmed of Yahweh
in a place on earth in the exile and post-exile. מכון appears in
Is 4:5 and Dn 8:11, יָשַׁב in Ps 9:12; 68:17; 132:13f, always with
reference to Jerusalem and the temple. Some would object against
the late dating of Ps 68:17, but it should be noted that the
verse in question has several exclusively late usages which are
also Aramaisms: גְּבֻנִּים is a hapax and an Aramaism; רצד
only appears elsewhere in Sir 14:22 and is an Aramaism[18].

Thus we can conclude that 1 Kg 8:13 is post-Deuteronomic
and uses a Deuteronomistic phrase in a manner that is beyond
the Deuteronomic formulation.

The same chain of reasoning applies to the the Song as well,
because Yahweh leads the people to his dwelling place, which is
some place on earth. The development that allows for the formulation מָכוֹן לְשִׁבְתְּךָ to be applied to the temple in both 1 Kg

---

8:13 and the Song occurs during the exile and post-exile. In Ugaritic mythology Jabal-al-Aqra, the highest mountain in northern Syria, is identified with the mythical residence of the gods. The temple in Ugarit is then seen to have a special relation to this residence[19]. From the exile on, the very high mythical mountain, the residence of the gods, their meeting place in the North, is appropriated into Israelite thought and applied to Zion, where Yahweh is seen to be permanently resident. Compare the place where the gods are seated on the mountain in the recesses of the North described in Is 14:13[20] with Ps 48:3[21], where Zion is the mountain of the recesses of the North, and with Ps 74:8, which terms the destroyed sanctuary "the meeting places of אֵל." The temple mountain becomes a very high mountain, Ezk 40:2, Ps 78:69, which is the highest of all mountains, Is 2:2[22] and its parallel Mic 4:1, and the true mountain residence of Yahweh, Ps 68:17. Jerusalem takes on the eternal fixity of the myth mountain, which is Yahweh's own proper residence, Ps 78:69; 125:1; 132:13f, and which is his inheritance, Ps 74:2[23].

Consonant with the application of myth forms to the manner of Yahweh's residence in Jerusalem is the notion that Yahweh

19 J. C. L. Gibson, *Canaanite Myths and Legends*, 2nd ed. (Edinburgh: T and T Clark, 1977) 7.
20 Despite attempts to style this an early passage only later adapted for use against Babylon, the natural placement of a description of the fall of Babylon the enemy is at the end of the exile or later; R. E. Clements, *Isaiah 1-39*, New Century Bible Commentary (Grand Rapids: Eerdmans, 1980) 140; Kaiser, *Isaiah 13-39* 32.
21 See my treatment below pp 170-174.
22 Clements 40.
23 There is agreement on the post-exilic nature of Ps 125, Ravasi 3:557. The opinion of the exegetes on Ps 132 is not as certain. Ravasi only admits a post-exilic adaptation, 3:669. But it is best to see it as a post-exilic composition asking for the restoration of the monarchy, vv 17f. See the cogent argument to that effect in Kirkpatrick 762-764; see also *The New Jerusalem Bible* note e to Ps 132:10, note h to 132:18, which argue for the period when the priest and the descendent of David were to rule together and both be anointed.

has himself built the sanctuary. In the Ugaritic myths the palace of the god becomes his permanent and unchangeable abode and the place from which he can rule forever because he has built it or caused it to be built. Thus the notion that Yahweh has built the temple, v 17a, b, and then rules from it forever, v 18, is very much entwined with the notion of Jerusalem being his own proper place of dwelling.

It is very problematic whether the notion that God builds either the city or the temple within it is present in any pre-exilic tradition. The earliest recorded tradition regarding the temple in Jerusalem does not approve of temple building, 2 Sm 7:5-7. Then 7:13, a later level of tradition, will affirm that Yahweh foretold that David's son would build the temple; see also 1 Kg 5:19; 8:19. But there is nothing there approaching the affirmation that Yahweh has built the temple. There is present a statement of fact, or at most a light statement of approval, but no real involvement on Yahweh's part.

In regard to the city in which the temple resides, it is very hard to reconcile the notion of God as its primordial founder with any period in the pre-exile because of the fact that David took over the city from non-Israelites, the Jebusites. The Jebusites were part of the indigenous population that Yahweh would expel, and it would not be possible to state that he was simply the builder of a city they had built.

It is also very difficult to reconcile a tradition of Yahweh as founder of the city with the refusal of Yahweh to have a permanent residence in Jerusalem in the early traditions. If there was a tradition that he had built the city, there would be no need to insist on the temporary nature of his residence there. The deity is supposed to have a permanent residence in the city that he has built. The insistence on portability would not be consonant with the notion that Yahweh was the original builder of Jerusalem.

In the pre-exile the city becomes the city of Yahweh and he has a special relation to it because of his temple there and because it is the city of the dynasty of David, which is his dynasty. These notions are especially prevalent in the Jerusalem theology of Isaiah. But Isaiah never arrives at a foundation myth, with God as the original builder of the city. God founds the city, but as the one who is with the city and gives it its present solidity and protection, Is 7:1-4; 37:35.

There are texts that are usually attributed to the period of Isaiah which use water myth images to portray the attacks against the city and how God will sustain it, Is 17:12-14; Ps 46. But the pre-exilic nature of both of these texts is disputed. Kaiser seems willing to accept the redactional nature of the Is text[24]. As regards Ps 46 there is no clear way to arrive at critical agreement. But even if the pre-exilic nature of both texts is granted, it does not follow from these texts themselves that they represent a foundation myth. All that is finally asserted here is the protection of the city. The city stands against the chaotic waters in both texts, but that motif in Isaiah does not carry with it the notion that Yahweh is the primordial founder. Isaiah has used water images and the notion of preservation from the destructive waters before, Is 8:7f, but all that he affirms is that the waters will not destroy the city. And in Ps 46 all that is affirmed of Yahweh is that he is strength, refuge, and with the city, that is, protector of the city.

In these texts there is the sense of present establishment of the city, sometimes using motifs from creation myths, but not the application of that myth to Yahweh in such a way as to affirm that he was the one who built the city and the temple.

The only text where you have an actual foundation word present is Is 14:32, "God has founded Zion." The pre-exilic

---

24 Kaiser, *Isaiah 13-39* 85f.

status of this texts is not questioned by the commentators[25]. But since they are to be placed in the period of Assyrian onslaught, then the use of יָסַד צִיּוֹן can reasonably be equated with its use in 28:16, that is, as a present act of protecting the city, not as some statement of a current foundation myth.

Other texts indicate that Yahweh has formed and made the events that result in the preservation of the city, Is 22:11; 37:26, and he has formed these events in ancient times. The authenticity of these texts is not usually accepted. Kaiser places both texts in the early exile[26]. But even here there is no statement of the creation of the city; they are still preservation statements. It is easy to see how one could then cross over from these statements to an affirmation that Yahweh has formed and made the city itself, but neither Isaiah or any other pre-exilic thinker has made the transition. Until the post-exile the original city of Jerusalem was one that men, not God built, see Jer 32:31, which speaks of God's wrath against the city which *they* built.

The idea that God builds city and temple is consonant with the restoration period because God is the primary builder in the reconstruction of the temple and Jerusalem. This seems to be a development starting within the exilic school of Isaiah and continuing into the post-exile. It is present in Is 2:2 and its parallel Mic 4:1, (see also Is 4:5); Is 26:1; 44:24-28; 54:11; 62:5-7 (your sons is normally emended to your builder, referring it to Yahweh); 65:18. It then also appears in texts very closely related to the Isaian school, Jer 30:18; 31:4.

It arises because of a developed sense of the control that Yahweh has over world events. Because he created all of these peoples, he alone has full disposition of their destinies, especially as they affect Israel and his plans for her. Thus Yahweh is the

25 Kaiser, *Isaiah 13-39* 51; Clements 148.
26 Kaiser, *Isaiah 13-39* 144, 396.

builder of Jerusalem because he controls the men and events that determine her restoration, Is 44:24-28; 45:13. And this restoration can be identified with his power to create, 45:12f, 18; 65:18. In a text closely related to the Isaian school, Jer 33:2, the notion that God was former and creator of events that was present in Is 22:11 and 37:26 in regard to the city's preservation, is now applied to the city's reconstruction, Jer 33:4-7.

The concept is that men and men's events result in the rebuilding, but that God is the ultimate builder. This notion of God controlling the whole course of events that concern the rebuilding runs all the way through the story of the reconstruction of both the second temple and the walls of the city of Jerusalem. Yahweh is the one ultimately responsible for the rescript of Cyrus allowing the rebuilding, because he gave Cyrus all the kingdoms of the earth and appointed him to build his house in Jerusalem, Ezr 1:2f. Also, he stirred up his spirit to promulgate the decree, 1:1, as well as the spirit of those who returned to rebuild, 1:5. The prophets of God impel the rebuilding after the project is stalled, 5:1, see Hag 1:8; 2:4; Zech 1:16; 6:12-15; 8:9. And this word again stirs up the spirit of the builders, Hag 1:14. The attempt to stop the building did not succeed because "the eye of God was on the elders of the Jews," Ezr 5:5, and they finished the building by the command of God, 6:14.

God is also responsible for the rebuilding of the walls of the city. Nehemiah prays to God before making his request to the king, Neh 1:11; 2:4. He receives the material because God's hand is on him, 2:8. God will bless the work, and those who build are his servants, 2:20. And finally, the completed construction of the walls is simply called "the work done by our God," 6:16. God is the builder of Jerusalem and its temple, elsewhere, only in Psalms of the exile and post-exile, Ps 48:9; 51:20; 69:36[27]; 87:5[28]; 102:17[29]; 147:2, 13.

Explicit description of the first foundation of the temple and city as having been carried out by Yahweh is only found in the Asaphite Ps 78:69. To arrive at this formulation, the psalm, like v 17 of the Song of the Sea, has recourse to myth formulations. He uses language current in the post-exilic world that pertains to God's creation and original establishment of the world and which gave it its present unending stability, and applies it to the foundation of the temple. See Am 9:6a, a late myth description of the foundation of the world[30], whose language is identical to that used for the foundation of the temple in Ps 78:69.

The conclusion is that the notion that God is the original maker of the sacred area, Jerusalem and its temple, is not consonant with the situation of the entire pre-exile. The development of the idea that God is builder of Jerusalem and the temple then follows the familiar pattern of a first formulation in the school of Dt-Is regarding the foreseen restoration and then application back to the beginning of things because the power that God evinces in the act of restoration is creative and so always was present. Then there is the arrival at the concept with all the marks that it has in the Song of the Sea only in the work of the Asaphites, Ps 78:69.

Excursus: The Placement of Ps 78

Ps 78 has a very close relationship of vocabulary, phrasing, and conceptualization with the Song of the Sea throughout parts one and two. This correspondence between the two pieces makes it important to identify the time and place of composition

27 Ravasi 2:407.
28 Ravasi 2:792f.
29 Ravasi 3:33-35.
30 Lindblom 117.

of Ps 78. Unfortunately, this psalm is famous for the general lack of critical agreement on its dating. Still, I maintain that there is sufficient evidence to place it in the post-exile.

Many indications regarding the dating have already emerged in the previous discussion. The idea that God is גּוֹאֵל of Israel, Ps 78:35, occurs in 31 instances other than here and the Song, all are exilic or post-exilic. מִקְדָּשׁ to designate the temple, v 69, appears 51 times outside of Ps 78 and the Song, all exilic or later. The notion that God builds the sanctuary and the identification of the sanctuary with God's proper residence are both confined elsewhere to the later periods, and to portray this Ps 78 uses a late myth statement found in Am 9:6. Israel portrayed as crossing, אָבַר, the Reed Sea, Ps 78:13, never appears in early texts. The Deuteronomistic text of Js 4:23 affirms that the Israelites crossed the Reed Sea. After that, the tradition element appears frequently. Perhaps it is present in the texts of Is 43:2, 16. It is certainly present in Is 51:10. It then appears in Ps 136:14; Neh 9:11; Nb 33:8. Also, the concept of crossing with the use of some other word is always late, Ps 106:9; Is 63:13; Ex 14:16, 22, 29 (all P[31]); 15:19, thus never before the exile.

That the waters split or were divided, Ps 78:13, never appears in early texts. It is probable that the idea begins in Is 51:9, which speaks of the primordial monster being cut to pieces. The notion of the waters being split is almost certainly present in Ps 74:13 and in 136:13. The term בָּקַע appears in Is 63:12 and then in the P editor of Ex 14, vv 16, 21.

Some commentators have expressed the opinion that this Psalm is of the period of David, or at least of the monarchy, because of the mention of David and the travels of the ark that eventually arrives in Jerusalem, vv 67-72[32]. But various authors

---

31 Kohata 372.
32 Cross, "Canaanite Myth" 134; Freedman, "Divine Names" 77-79.

have noted that the rendition of Israelite history here is called a מָשָׁל, a comparison, v 2. And they have proposed that the story told here of the rejection of Shiloh and the choosing of Zion and David is a parable to explain the post-exilic period of antipathy toward the Samaritans and to prove that the temple in Jerusalem is the true one and that Samaritan worship is not[33].

This insight is the key to the correct interpretation of the Psalm. It is a characteristic of the Asaphites that they like to explain a present situation by showing how it is either based in some very ancient event or how it recapitulates a base event; what happened then is happening now. The present disposition of the temple in Ps 74:1-11 is based within the action of God at the exodus. The resolution of the present unidentified difficulty of Ps 77:2-13 is to be found in the exodus event, vv 14-21. The present state of ruin of the city of Jerusalem and its walls, Ps 80:13f, is compared to the days of the conquest when it was established, vv 9-12. The conspiracy of the surrounding peoples in Ps 83:2-9 uses ancient names of peoples now long gone, and God is asked to act now as he acted in ancient times against the peoples who then inhabited those areas, vv 10-12. For the Asaphites there is the overall notion that base events are redone, and appreciation of them is the key to the present situation.

We can demonstrate what the present situation is that the psalmist is referring to by examining his use of Deuteronomic material. Many have noted that Ps 78 is highly Deuteronomic in its language[34]. But its real relationship is to late Deuteronomistic redactors. Note these Deuteronomistic clichés[35] that do not appear in pre-Deuteronomistic material:

---

33 Ravasi 2:620.
34 Foresti 55-58.
35 Weinfeld 365.

78:8, סֹרֵר מוֹרֶה לֵב: Jer 5:13.

78:10, הָלַך בְּתוֹרַת: 2 Kg 10:31; Jer 9:13; 26:4; 32:23; 44:10, 23.

78:43, אֹתוֹת וּמוֹפְתִים: Dt 4:31; 6:22; 7:19; 26:8; 29:2; 34:11; Jer 32:20f.

78:56, שָׁמַר עֵדוֹת: Dt 6:17, 1 Kg 2:3; 2 Kg 17:15; 23:3.

78:70, בָּחַר בְּדָוִד עַבְדּוֹ: 1 Kg 8:16, 11:34.

The specific description of the rejection of Israel in the time of the Judges is portrayed in terms that are particularly Deuteronomistic. כעס, provoke, v 58, of Israel provoking God, is found 23 times throughout the Deuteronomic corpus and is markedly, and likely exclusively, Deuteronomistic: Dt 4:25; 9:18; 31:29; 32:16, 21; Jg 2:12; 1 Kg 14:9, 15; 15:30; 16:2, 7, 13, 26, 33; 21:22; 22:54; 2 Kg 17:11, 17; 21:6, 15; 22:17; 23:19; Jer 7:18, 19; 8:19; 11:17; 25:6, 7; 32:29, 30, 32; 44:3, 8. And this particular formulation of provoking God with פְּסִילִים, idols, is found only in the late Deuteronomistic level, Dt 4:25, and a redactive addition to Jer, 8:19[36]. קנא, make jealous, of man making God jealous is only of the Deuteronomistic school, see Dt 32:16, 21; 1 Kg 14;22[37]. .

In Ps 78:59, 60 God grows angry, rejects Israel, and forsakes the shrine at Shiloh. The succession of words used is הִתְעַבֵּר, נָטַשׁ, מָאַס. This whole vocabulary is very Deuteronomistic, and this description of the whole course of events is according to the thought of Jeremiah's redactors. The depiction of God's anger using the specific verbal הִתְעַבֵּר form only occurs in Dt 3:26, a Deuteronomistic passage. God's rejection of Israel with the use of מָאַס appears in the late Jer 6:30[38]. Then the whole

---

36 Carroll 236.

37 John Gray, *1 and 2 Kings*, Old Testament Library (Philadelphia: Westminster, 1970) 340.

38 Carroll 204.

phrasing of 59b, בְּיִשְׂרָאֵל ... וַיִּמְאַס, can be compared to the Deuteronomistic redactor in 2 Kg 17:20[39]. נטשׁ, predicated of God leaving Israel, is also characteristic of the Deuteronomic corpus, Jg 6:13; 1 Sm 12:22; 2 Kg 21:14; Jer 7:29; 23:33, 39. But the whole rejection vocabulary, מאס, נטשׁ, and עבר, appears together only in Jer 7:29b, an editorial addition[40].

The description of God leaving his shrine at Shiloh is composed entirely of usages restricted to the book of Jer that regard the shrines at Shiloh and Jerusalem. The description of the Shrine at Shiloh as a place where God resides, שׁכן, is only found in a clearly Deuteronomistic text of Jeremiah, 7:12[41]. The redactor equates the fate of the shrine at Jerusalem with the shrine at Shiloh, 7:14; 26:6, 9, all Deuteronomistic texts[42]. Then the use of נטשׁ for God abandoning his sanctuary (now Jerusalem) only occurs in Jer 12:7, a text not earlier than the fall of the city[43].

But in Ps 78 we find that by v 67 God has not really rejected all of Israel, only the northern tribes and their shrine. He has in fact not rejected the tribe of Judah, v 68, nor Zion. That can be compared to the supplication of the redactor in Jer 14:19[44] that Judah and Zion be not rejected. In v 70 we find that Yahweh's servant David has not been rejected. That can be compared with the certainty of the book of consolations of Jeremiah that David, the servant of Yahweh, has not been rejected, Jer 33:26.

The whole of the picture is according to the mentality of the redactors of the book of Jeremiah basing themselves on Deuteronomistic thought.

---

39 Gray , *Kings* 649.
40 Carroll 219.
41 Carroll 209f.
42 Carroll 209f, 515.
43 Carroll 290.
44 Carroll 318.

The picture of Ps 78 that emerges then supports the מָשָׁל theory. The author is writing on the historical level to tell the story of the loss of the ark at Shiloh and its recovery, but in such a way as to portray the exile, שְׁבִי, v 61, and the restoration of the temple, vv 69f, along with the statement that the Samaritans have been rejected by God, v 67. He uses primarily Deuteronomistic material, but in a post-Deuteronomic manner. He wants to display how the present post-exilic situation has its foundation already present in the beginning events.

This proposition also stands out sharply if we return to the strong similarities that we have noted between Ps 78 and Ps 74. Ps 74 also wants to explain the present situation of the temple by recourse to the foundation events. The hope of the rebuilding of the temple rests on the acts of God at the exodus. In these psalms the description of the temple site is so close as to indicate that they were very likely written in the same period and come from the same school, if not the same author. We have already compared 78:54, 68 with 74:2, and 78:52 with 74:1b. The מִקְדָּשׁ, in a state of ruin in 74:7, is standing in 78:69. Thus, some time after the rebuilding of the temple would be indicated for the placement of Ps 78.

The above has confirmation in the fact that the Psalm has Dt-Isaian, Tr-Isaian, and other post-exilic material related to the Isaian school, in the descriptions of the exodus. The depiction of the water in the desert is identical to the usage that is found in Dt-Is:

יִבַּקַע צֻרִים	Ps 78:15		וַיָּזוּבוּ מַיִם	Ps 78:20
וַיִּבְקַע־צוּר	Is 48:21ba		וַיָּזֻבוּ מָיִם	Is 48:21bβ

Or the elements of the description in 78:16 can be compared to Is 48:21a:

Is 48:21a   מַיִם צוּר, הִזִּיל

Ps 78:16   מַיִם סֶלַע, נוֹזְלִים

The language of Is 43:20 has certainly influenced Ps 78:15, 16 in its vocabulary and presentation:

Is 43:20b   בַּמִּדְבָּר מַיִם, נְהָרוֹת, לְהַשְׁקוֹת

Ps 78:15f   בַּמִּדְבָּר מָיִם, נְהָרוֹת, וַיַּשְׁקְ

The above texts from Ps 78 can also be compared with Is 35:6b.

The depiction of the crossing of the sea in v 13a is of the general Dt-Isaian form; see Is 51:10b.

Then the bringing into the land, 78:54f, is of the same form as the return described in Is 56:6 and a text from the same moment of redaction, 57:13. Compare:

Ps 78:54	וַיְבִיא	ם	אֶל־גְּבוּל	קָדְשׁוֹ הַר...
78:55				נַחֲלָה
Is 56:7	וַהֲבִיאוֹתִי ם	אֶל־הַר	קָדְשׁי	
57:13	יִנְחַל	...	הַר	קָדְשׁי

The formulations are identical when it is taken into account that גְּבוּל and הַר are in parallelism in Ps 78:54.

Ps 78:40 says that the Israelites rebelled and provoked God in the desert. This can be compared to Is 63:10 where the Israelites have rebelled and provoked God's holy spirit. These are the only places in Scripture where the combination of vocabulary is used.

Also the lament for the ark, Ps 78:61-63, can profitably be compared to the lament for the destroyed temple in Is 64:10.

In Ps 78:52 God has lead the people like a flock in the desert; compare that to Is 63:3; Ps 136:16; 106:9:

וַיַּסַּע כַּצֹּאן עַמּוֹ וַיְנַהֲגֵם כָּעֵדֶר בַּמִּדְבָּר　Ps 78:52

מוֹלִיכָם בַּתְּהֹמוֹת כַּסּוּס בַּמִּדְבָּר　Is 63:13

לְמוֹלִיךְ עַמּוֹ בַּמִּדְבָּר　Ps 136:16

וַיּוֹלִיכֵם בַּתְּהֹמוֹת כַּ מִדְבָּר　Ps 106:9

The phrase looks suspiciously like a format that was used with variations in the post-exilic temple.

That notion of passage in the desert is followed by the statement that they did not fear, Ps 78:53. This is an exact duplicate of Is 12:2. Compare:

לָבֶטַח וְלֹא פָחָדוּ　Ps 78:53
אֶבְטַח וְלֹא אֶפְחָד　Is 12:2a

It is then very important to note that as Ps 78:53 comes after the theme of the leading in the desert of v 52; so also Is 12:2, in the redactive scheme of the book, comes directly after a late passage dealing with the highway for the returnees, which is likened to the highway that was there at the time of the exodus, Is 11:16. Such consonance of thought dictates a similarity of milieu.

Thus, Ps 78 can be firmly placed in the post-exile. The statement of the solidity of the sanctuary would indicate some time after the completion of the building of the temple. It can be noted that the sons of Asaph, the composers of Ps 78, were present at the laying of the cornerstone of the temple of God, Ezr 3:10f, and this action of the builders, בֹּנִים, was described with the verb יָסַד, to found. According to the principle, work of man, work of God, the same action is ascribed to God who builds, בָּנָה, and founds, יָסַד, his temple in Ps 78:69. The separation of the Samaritans from the cult was established during this building period, Ezr 4:1-3. The celebration of the dynasty of David, vv 70-72, concurs with the Messianic expectations that were current during and after the rebuilding of the temple, Hag 2:23; Zech 4:14; Jer 33:21f, 26.

The Fear of the Peoples, vv 14-16

In terms of tradition development, this part of the poem can, like the first part, be identified as post-Deuteronomic. First, vv 14-16 have a very strong verbal and conceptual relationship with a series of texts involved in the Deuteronomistic account of the arrival at and entrance into the holy land. The texts involved are Dt 2:25-29;11:25; Js 2:9-11, 24; 4:22-5:1, Ex 23:27. Compare:

14שָׁמְעוּ עַמִּים יִרְגָּזוּן חִיל	הָעַמִּים...יִשְׁמְעוּן...רָגְזוּ וְחָלוּ	Dt 2:25
15 נָמֹגוּ כֹּל יֹשְׁבֵי כְנָעַן	נָמֹגוּ כָּל־יֹשְׁבֵי הָאָרֶץ	Js 2:9
	נָמֹגוּ כָּל־יֹשְׁבֵי הָאָרֶץ	2:24
16 תִּפֹּל עֲלֵיהֶם אֵימָתָה	נָפְלָה אֵימַתְכֶם עָלֵינוּ	2:9
	אֵימָתִי ... כָּל־הָעָם	Ex 23:27
וָפַחַד	פַּחְדְּךָ	Dt 2:25
	פַּחְדְּכֶם	11:25
עַד־יַעֲבֹר ... עַד־יַעֲבֹר	עַד־עָבְרְכֶם ... עַד־עָבְרֵנוּ	Js 4:23
	עַד־עָבְרֵנוּ (כתיב)	5:1
	אֶעְבְּרָה ... אֶעְבְּרָה	Dt 2:27f
	עַד ... אֶעֱבֹר	29f

We note that the D texts all come from within very late redactional levels. They interlock and were made to do so either by the last Deuteronomistic editors or the post Deuteronomic editors. In Dt 2:24aβb, 25[45] it states that God will give Israel

---

45 Mayes, *Deuteronomy* 134.

the land of the Amorite king, Sihon. This victory will be followed by one over Og, 3:1ff. These victories are accompanied by a holy war oracle. Not only does God promise victory in the present campaigns, but he also promises that these campaigns will begin to instill divine fear into the other peoples to be conquered, (see also the Deuteronomistic texts, Ex 23:27; Dt 11:25[46]). This oracle is verified in the late Deuteronomistic speech of Rahab, Js 2:9[47], because she states that the divine fear has fallen on the dwellers of the land because they have heard what the Israelites did to the Amorite kings, Js 2:10. The two texts really have to be of the same level of redaction, which is either late Deuteronomistic or post-Deuteronomic, for the Dt text states that God will begin to instill fear; therefore its accomplishment is inferred. The Js text verifies that it has been accomplished. The text of Js 2:24 is then an exact repetition of 2:9b and simply verifies to Joshua that the people really are in terror. Then the Deuteronomistic Js 4:22-5:1[48] is clearly of a piece with 2:10f. The drying of the Reed Sea, 4:23, is of the same hand as 2:10a, and the fear of the peoples in the cis-Jordan in 5:1 is a virtual duplicate of 2:11a.

The whole set of texts wishes to establish that everything that is to happen under Joshua is either a redoing of something that has happened under Moses, or is the continuation and result of something begun under Moses, either in the trans-Jordan or in the exodus. The crossing of the Jordan is a redoing of the Reed Sea crossing and continues to instill the fear that the Reed Sea crossing did, Js 2:9f; 4:22-5:1. The conquest of

---

46 Mayes, *Deuteronomy* 207f. The text is Deuteronomistic.

47 Trent C. Butler, *Joshua*, Word Biblical Commentary 17 (Waco: Word Books, 1983) 31. John Gray, *Joshua, Judges, Ruth*, New Century Bible Commentary (Grand Rapids: Eerdmans, 1986) 65. That Js 2:9-11 is Deuteronomistic is the common opinion of recent commentators.

48 The language is archetypically Deuteronomistic, Butler, *Joshua* 41, cf Weinfeld 332 par 3; 333 par 3b; 344 par 15; 358 par 15.

Jericho continues the conquest begun by Moses in the trans-Jordan and is a result of the terror begun by him, Js 2:9-11.

In addition to the very strong agreement of phrasing demonstrated in the chart above, there are points of conceptual agreement that are shared only by vv 14-16 of the Song and these Deuteronomistic texts. V 16b of the Song uses the phrase עַד־עָבַר to describe the crossing into the Holy Land, because the phrase continues v 13 which had brought them to the edge of the Holy Land and results in their being brought in, v 17. But the same phrase also describes the passage through the surrounding peoples on their approach. The peoples of Edom, Moab and Philistia are described as immobilized until the Israelites pass through. Thus the one phrase indicates both the passage through the surrounding peoples and the transit of the Jordan.

The Deuteronomistic text also has a similar point of view. The petition to pass through the land of Sihon uses the word עָבַר in such a way so as to indicate one sweep of passage through the land, specifically Edom, and through the Jordan, Dt 2:27-30. But the notion hinges not on the text as a whole but on one verse, Dt 2:29. For it is there that Moses tells Sihon that his request that he let the Sons of Israel cross his land is "as Edom... and the Moabites... did, until I cross the Jordan." Without this verse the account would not even speak of a crossing through Edom, Moab or the Jordan. With it, עד עבר specifies both the passage through Edom and Moab, to which it looks back, and the crossing of the Jordan which it foresees. It is specifically Dt 2:29 that brings the account to the same conceptual level that we find in the Song. Now Dt 2:29 is an addition of the post-Deuteronomic Levites[49], and it is therefore to them that we must look for the mentality of the rendition in our piece.

49 Mayes, *Deuteronomy* 134.

Also, the testimony of Rahab states that the people are afraid because they have "heard" what God did at the Reed Sea, Js 2:10. Now that is the exact conceptual duplicate of v 14, the peoples fear because they heard what God did at the Reed Sea.

Also, the peoples of the cis-Jordan too are in fear because Yahweh dried up the Jordan "until the Israelites crossed over," Js 5:1. And this is also what is portrayed in the vv 15b, 16 of the Song; the dwellers of Canaan are in fear until the Israelites cross over the Jordan, v 16b, and into the holy land, v 17.

The overall similarities between vv 14-16 of the Song text and these texts are so great that there has to be some line of influence between the two. It remains to be established which way this line stretches.

The ensemble of fear texts revolves around the speech of Rahab, and the dating of that text can established with a considerable degree of certitude. Her speech is imbued with the theology of the Deuteronomistic redactor[50]. Js 2:9a, 11b can be compared to Dt 4:38, 39. That latter passage is integral to a discourse that includes a description of the exile and hope of return, Dt 4:27-31[51]. It is probable that this whole level of redaction sees the original entrance into the Holy Land as the basis for the re-entrance involved in the return and should be placed no earlier than the late exile, when there reappeared the real prospect for restoration to the land.

The text of the Song relates to these Deuteronomistic texts and to the post-Deuteronomic texts mentioned above, never to any motif that is pre-Deuteronomistic. It is extremely difficult to imagine a set of circumstances that would allow that the Song texts be before the Deuteronomistic redactor.

---

50 *The New Jerusalem Bible* note c to Js 2:11.
51 Moran 257 par g.

We can confirm this by the following: V 16 of the Song represents that the Israelites were able to pass, עָבַר, through the surrounding peoples at the time of their approach to the Holy Land. If we examine the JE traditions concerning the approach to the Holy Land, we can note that passing, עָבַר, is denied to the Israelites, Nb 20:14-21, especially v 21. They are forced to go around, סָבַב, Edom, 21:4. This same formulation is still found within the framework of D, in the text of Jg 11:15-18. Israel may not pass through Edom and Moab, v 17, but it does go around them, v 18. This text of Jg is Deuteronomistic in language[52], so late pre-exilic at the earliest[53].

But when you get to the exilic Deuteronomistic historian there is an exact reversal of the formulation. סָבַב is denied of the Israelites, Dt 2:3, and עָבַר is affirmed, Dt 2:4. The Israelites are able to pass through both the territories of Edom and Moab, 2:8f, 28f.

This formulation is found elsewhere in Dt 29:15; Js 24:17. Dt 29:15 is from the exilic Deuteronomistic redactor also[54]. The use of stone and wood for idols, 29:16, is found elsewhere in Dt in the already mentioned exilic text of 4:28, and in 28:36, 64, which also speaks clearly of the situation in exile. Elsewhere the phrase is used only by the Deuteronomistic redactor, 2 Kg 19:18[55] = Is 37:19, and in Ezk 20:32. It is clear that the text is from the exilic redaction of Dt and really expresses the situation of the exiles in the midst of nations that worship idols, and who must keep themselves uncontaminated, and keep alive the hope of return. Js 24:17 is part of a work that all agree has

---

52 Gray, *Joshua* 316.
53 See De Vaux, *Early History* 2:821, who summarizes a different point of view but arrives at the same time period..
54 Mayes, *Story* 46.
55 Gwilym H. Jones *1 and 2 Kings*, vol 2, New Century Bible Commentary (Grand Rapids: Eerdmans, 1984) 577.

gone through an extensive post-Deuteronomic redaction. This text is a duplicate of Dt 29:15 and can thus be presumed to be part of that redaction.

Beyond this, it is certain that all of the above passing texts are not before the exile, because the new formulation rests on a changed geopolitical situation that only arose at the exile. Starting then and continuing in the post-exile, the Edomites crossed over and settled in the western side of the Arabah, and their holdings extended to the Gulf of Aqaba. There is no possible way to go around Edom any more when viewed from the geographical situation existing from the exile onwards. Hence the exilic Deuteronomistic school formulates the tradition so that the Israelites pass through the Edomites and Moabites[56].

The same principle is valid for the Song because it represents the Israelites passing through the peoples, including the Edomites and Moabites. The formulation of v 16 cannot be before the political change that occurred during the exilic period. Nor can the Song be exilic; for it is clearly cultic of temple entrance and shows usages that are only explainable by active cultic use. Thus, it must be after the late Deuteronomistic and post-Deuteronomic Levitical editions and based on it.

We can further confirm this by a continued examination of the arrival and entrance tradition as they occur in the Song. It presents us with both the Canaanites and the surrounding peoples being subject to a fear that comes from hearing what God did. The language is that of the holy war and speaks of a divine fear. Neither this concept of the divine fear preceding the Israelites nor an oracle announcing it is anywhere present in the JE traditions, not in regard to the Canaanites, not in regard to the surrounding peoples. And the tradition in regard to the surrounding peoples is the opposite of the divine fear. God

56 *The New Jerusalem Bible* note a to Dt 2.

leads the Israelites away from the land of the Philistines so that the Israelites will not be disheartened, and turn back to Egypt, Ex 13:17, 18a (E[57]). The reference to the Philistines is anachronistic; still, the only tradition in regard to this geographical area is the exact opposite of what is represented in the Song.

Also, in regard to Edom the tradition is one of no fear on the part of the Edomites, and it is the Israelites who depart when their peaceful request for passage is denied, Nb 20:14-21 (generally held to be E[58]).

Moab does fear before the Israelites, Nb 22:2, and there is a divine vision of future Israelite victories, Nb 24:7-9, 15-18. Still, in none of this is there any sense of fear instilled by God, nor is there the form of a war oracle, nor is there any relation to the vocabulary of vv 14-16 of the Song.

It is only with the Deuteronomistic redactors where you have the oracle of the divine fear that will precede the Israelites. But in the their formulation this fear only affects the Canaanites, never the surrounding peoples.

In regard to Edom and Moab the earlier Deuteronomistic redactors simply state, like JE, that there was no divine fear present, and that Edom and Moab did not allow the Israelites to pass, and that the Israelites moved back, Jg 11:16ff.

When you get to the later Deuteronomistic levels there are some of the elements of the Song present but a very different formulation of these elements. In their account the Edomites do fear the Israelites, but not by a divine act, Dt 2:4. There is a war oracle form directed towards Edom and Moab, but it is the opposite of that of the Song; the Israelites are not to disturb either of these peoples because it is God himself who has given

---

57 Kohata 372.
58 N. H. Snaith, *Leviticus and Numbers*, The Century Bible, (London: Nelson, 1967) 276f.

them their land, and the Israelites will not receive any of it, Dt 2:4f, 9.

The real relation of the Song's fear of the surrounding peoples text is to the D tradition, but it cannot be placed within that tradition nor its development from its sources. The JE tradition rests in the event and the Deuteronomistic text of Jg 11:16ff takes over the JE telling of that event, only adding the Moabites to the Edomites as having refused passage. The exilic Deuteronomist then adds an oracle forbidding warfare because he has the Israelites passing through their land.

Nor can the Song be a parallel development; it is far to close to the whole Deuteronomistic configuration. And a parallel development that simply contradicts the main point of the tradition, that the Israelites had no mandate from God in the form of a holy war oracle in regard to these countries, is hard to conceive. And if we are to admit any progression at all in the fear of the peoples tradition, then the progression clearly points to a post-Deuteronomic time. The Song text has to be a use of that tradition that is posterior to it. The entrance that the text is expressing would then have to demonstrate the attitudes surrounding a post-Deuteronomic entrance into the Holy Land. That has to be the return from the Babylonian exile.

And, in fact, texts that speak of the fear of the surrounding peoples upon the entrance of the Israelites are limited to the post-exilic redactors of the prophets and regard the return: Jer 33:9 and Mic 7:17.

Jer 33:9 has the basic form of the Song. The nations "hear" about what God has done for Israel and they will fear and tremble, פָּחֲדוּ וְרָגְזוּ, because of it. There is an entrance implicitly spoken of because the people will fear upon the return of the Israelites, 33:7. It is also in the context of God rebuilding the city, 33:2-7. So that it has points of correspondence to all of the themes of vv 13-18. This text belongs to a redactive layer that is after the Deuteronomistic redactor of Jer and is post-exilic[59]. It is obviously part of the efforts to rebuild the city, including the rebuilding of the walls.

Another text that has the peoples fearing, יִפְחָדוּ ... יִרְגָּזוּ, upon the entrance of the Israelites is Mic 7:17. The entrance that he is speaking of is the return, 7:15, but he consciously equates the return with the exodus from Egypt and he describes that in pastoral terms, 7:14. And the peoples will fear when they perceive that God has performed this new exodus, 7:16. Thus, the general situation of vv 13-16 of the Song is present. There is no widely held opinion regarding the further precision of the Micah text beyond the fact that it is post-exilic[60].

We can therefore conclude that the initial entrance that is being described in the Song of the Sea is being done in such a way as to reflect the period of the return and the attitude towards the surrounding peoples to be found in that period.

The Asaphite nature of the entrance fear tradition

When we examine the phrasing present in the fear passage of the Song, we find that when the specific phrasing appears outside of the D source material, it always and only appears in Asaphite psalms. We found that v 15b was based on Js 2:9. The phrasing of the latter text is reproduced in Ps 75:4, נְמֹגִים אֶרֶץ וְכָל-יֹשְׁבֶיהָ. The poetic mentality of v 16aα of the Song, תִּפֹּל עֲלֵיהֶם פַּחַד, is already found in an early passage in the D corpus, 1 Sm 11:7b, but its use after D is restricted to the school of Asaph, Ps 105:38b. The word pair in v 16aβ of the Song, בִּגְדֹל זְרוֹעֲךָ, in the strength of your arm, is certainly

---

59 Carroll 635.
60 Mays 158.

influenced by D usages. The use of גדל as a noun form is one
of D's characteristics[61]. The texture of this phrasing begins to
appear, however, with the Deuteronomistic redactor; see Dt
11:2, וּזְרֹעוֹ ... גָדְלֹו. Then the specific expression that we have
in the Song only is found in the Asaphite Ps 79:11.

On the overall conceptual level this interlude is also traceable
to the sphere of the Sons of Asaph. The notion of an antagonistic
war oracle delivered against the people of Edom and Moab is
only verifiable of the Asaphites in the post-Deuteronomic literary
period. 2 Chr 20:14-17 represents Jehaziel, one of the Sons of
Asaph, delivering a war oracle against the peoples of the trans-
Jordan, v 10. The point of view displayed is that the victory
that God is about to carry out is a redoing of the victory of God
at the Reed Sea. 20:17 is a virtual repetition of Ex 14:13, when
Moses gives the war oracle that Yahweh will defeat the Egyptians.
So, in this manner Jehaziel takes the part of Moses at the Reed
Sea and equates victory here with victory over the Egyptians at
the Sea.

Such is the point of view of the composers of the Song. The
war oracle is delivered by Moses that the people that surround
Israel will be helpless before God. And the Song sees the victory
over the peoples as a repeat of the Reed Sea victory, because in
the description of the final defeat of the peoples in v 16a of the
Song it says that before God they have become like a stone.
That is the same description that is used for the final defeat of
the Egyptians at the hand of God, v 5. See also the equivalent
expression in v 10b.

Thus, all of the phrasing and the entire concept involved in
the fear of the people's section is traceable to the Asaphites and
to the Asaphites alone.

---

61 Tournay 353.

The Song and Ps 48

Ps 48 as a whole also has a linguistic and conceptual relation
to the Song. The fear words of 14b, 15 appear together in Ps
48:6f. Also, in Ps 48 the peoples are helpless against Zion, v
3a, the holy mountain, v 2, which is identified with the mythical
residence of God, v 3a, where he is king, v 3b, which he establishes
forever, v 9b. That can be compared with the helplessness of
the surrounding peoples, Ex 15:14-16, as God leads the people
to his holy abode, v 13, which is his mountain, v 17a, and is
his myth residence, v 17, which he establishes, 17b, and where
he is king forever, v 18.

The relation between the Song and Ps 48 is not one where
there is the same mind. The vocabulary usage and concepts
are similar, but there is no agreement in phrasing. Nor are we
in the same tradition. In Ps 48 the peoples have tried to attack
the city that God has built. Thus the psalm is representative of
the themes of the conspiracy of the peoples and the inviolability
of the city. In the Song the peoples are helpless as the Israelites
enter into the sanctuary that God has built. The notion of their
conspiracy and attack against the city and the city's inviolability
from that attack is not present.

Still, it is easy to see that the placement of Ps 48 is valuable
for our discussion. The Song of the Sea represents a situation
in which God has immobilized the peoples so that they cannot
act against his own people and their future residence in his
own holy dwelling. The situations of Ps 48 and the Song have
similar elements.

There is no critical agreement regarding the dating of Ps 48;
still, I hold that there is sufficient reason for placing the psalm
at the time of Nehemiah's project. Vv 13f speak of a celebration
of what are obviously the physical walls of Jerusalem on the

occasion of the defeat of some enemy who has never even arrived at the city to attack it, vv 5-7. Many critics have reasonably pointed out that the general situation where the enemy never is able to even mount the attack against the city fits very well with the invasion of Sennacherib in 701, or better, with the occasion of the Syro-Ephraimite war of 735[62].

Although a reference to the preservation of the city at the time of Isaiah is probably not absent from the mind of the author, it is very difficult to attribute the actual composition of this work to that period. The psalm considers that Yahweh is so much involved with the walls and the excellence of their construction that the walls can simply be termed, "this is Yahweh our God forever," v 15a.

Now the only record we have of the events of 735 and 701 indicates that Yahweh was not involved with the repair of the walls in the face of an imminent attack. In fact, there is friction between the act of rebuilding the walls and the policy of Yahweh. In Is 7:3 the prophet meets Ahaz as he is inspecting the water supply just outside the walls and considering its defenses. The policy that God commands is total trust, and the attitude that the king evinces during the inspection is counter the policy of God. One does not get the impression of any sympathy or interest of the prophet of God in any fortification project.

This attitude is much more clearly present during the siege of Sennacherib. God looks with disfavor on Hezekiah's policy of redoing the fortifications, Is 22:10ff. 22:10, 11a talks about the fortification efforts. Then 22:11b states, "But you have not looked to its maker and its former; you did not see it from long ago." This verse is telling the Israelites that they have not understood the events that God had formed and made long ago; therefore, their actions regarding the defensive measures had nothing to

---

62 Ravasi 1:855.

do with God's plan. Kaiser holds that 22:11b is not authentic and places it in the exile[63]. But even without that statement it is clear from 22:12-14 that God has no sympathy for the project, and certainly is in no way involved in it. It is very clear that Yahweh will save the city with no reference to its walls. A celebration of a victory where Yahweh is most intimately involved with the walls is not properly placed in this era.

I believe that Kaiser is correct when he states that 22:11b is exilic. This would indicate that the notion of God's lack of sympathy for the strengthening of the walls has to have carried on until that period. It is not until the late exile and the post-exile that there is the attitude that God wants the walls to be built up, to the extent that he is intimately involved in the project. The whole episode of Is 22:10ff then reappears in Jer 33:2-7. Is 22:10 speaks of the houses that were torn down to fortify the walls against the attacking Assyrians. That wall was eventually destroyed by the Babylonians. But those houses that were torn down and the walls to which the Babylonians laid siege reappear in Jer 33:4. And the description of Yahweh as the former and maker of the event found in Is 22:11b also reappears with it, Jer 33:2. But the mind of the post-exile has changed. The houses, and the walls that the kings of Judah had used them to fortify, will be rebuilt, and Yahweh is the framer of the events that will result in this project being carried out, 33:2-7.

The phrasing of Jer 33:2 repeats Is 22:11b and then adds that Yahweh establishes it (Jerusalem) and uses the word כוּן to portray the image. That can be compared with Ps 48:9b. Also, when God has carried out his plans, the nations that hear about it, אֲשֶׁר יִשְׁמָעוּ, fear and tremble, Jer 33:9. That can be compared with Ps 48:6f where the people are overcome when they see the city of God. Or the phrasing can be compared

---

63 Kaiser, *Isaiah 13-39* 144f.

to the marvel of the worshipers, or perhaps the attackers, when they hear, כַּאֲשֶׁר שָׁמַעְנוּ, about the city of God, v 9.

The language of Ps 48 as a whole is closely related to the late apocalypse found in Is 33, which also celebrates the inviolability of the city. Compare Is 33:5bα and Ps 48:11b, Is 33:14a and Ps 48:7a, Is 33:17a and Ps 48:3, Is 33:18b and Ps 48:13b, Is 33:20a and Ps 48:3.

Furthermore, the course of events in psalm 48 corresponds very well to the sequence of events and the outlook demonstrated in the rebuilding of the walls as told in Neh 4-6. The scene where the enemies conspire and advance against Jerusalem but never are able to mount the attack, Ps 48:5-9, corresponds to Neh 4:2, 9. Also compare the description of the machinations of the leaders of the surrounding peoples as they conspire to attack Jerusalem, Ps 48:5, נוֹעֲדוּ ... יַחְדָּו, with the conspiratorial actions of the enemies of the rebuilding as they plan together, יַחְדָּו, to attack the city, Neh 4:2, and where they seek to trap Nehemiah by inviting him to meet together with them, וְנִוָּעֲדָה יַחְדָּו , 6:2.

In the Nehemiah account there is a very strong identification of Yahweh with the walls that are rebuilt, Neh 6:16b; in Ps 48:5 the city and its walls are simply called "God our God." Then the psalm represents a procession around the city that celebrates their completion, 48:12-14, and such a procession went around the city to dedicate the walls in Neh 12:27-43. So a celebration involving a procession around the city in which a complete victory over the enemy is indicated and in which the walls are celebrated as the establishment of Yahweh, has all the require-ments of an event in the time of Nehemiah, and only in the time of Nehemiah.

Then, the climax of the Psalm, 48:8, כַּאֲשֶׁר שָׁמַעְנוּ ... רָאִינוּ, has a strong correspondence to the climax of the Nehemiah account of the successful rebuilding in the face of the surrounding peoples, Neh 6:16a, כַּאֲשֶׁר שָׁמְעוּ ... וַיִּרְאוּ. If Ps 48:8 means to include the attackers among those who marvel at the city and its walls that are being celebrated, then it has a very close conceptual correspondence to Neh 6:16. In any case, there is a clear correspondence of confessional language, and despite the three very common word involved, these are the only two places in Scripture with phrasing of this type.

It can then be noted that Neh 6:16 is the same verse that supplied the central line to Ps 118, a psalm which showed very strong indication of being from the immediate context of the rebuilding of the walls. Neh 6:16b corresponds to Ps 118:23f (pp 64f above). The verses in question, Ps 48:8; 118:23f; Neh 6:16, provide the climactic moment within their respective works. Also, all three verses are the moment which affirms the success of God's establishment of the walls of Jerusalem. One has the impression of being within a current of thought regarding the rebuilding and its effect on the surrounding peoples.

It can be concluded that there is sufficient evidence to place Ps 48 at the time of the successful rebuilding of the walls of the city of Jerusalem in the face of the conspiracy of the surrounding peoples who tried to stop the project.

The Song celebrates the entrance of the people into the holy place that God built, v 17. If we are in the post-exile, where the work of man is the work of God in the rebuilding projects, then entrance into the sanctuary that God has built would presuppose the building of that sanctuary by man. Thus, the Song would indicate that the surrounding peoples have been unable to prevent the rebuilding. That set of circumstances describes the period at and after the rebuilding of the walls by Nehemiah.

CHAPTER SIX
CONCLUSIONS

The Dating of the Song of the Sea

It can be granted that the Song of the Sea is of post-exilic provenience and that it has to come after the rebuilding of the temple. But the question remains, is the building referred to in Ex 15:17 the temple only or also Jerusalem and its walls? Is the time of composition sometime after the rebuilding of the temple or after the rebuilding of the walls?

The picture portrayed is that the people enter the Holy Land and also enter the sanctuary that God has built. Entering the sanctuary entails its first being built. The picture that results is that the entering and the building are seen as one continuous action. This picture applies well to the scene of the first returnees entering the Holy Land; they come back to build. They have the assurance of the rescript of Cyrus for the rebuilding of the temple, Ezr 1:1-4[1]. But the same can be said for the project of rebuilding the walls; Nehemiah returns with the rescript for the repair, Neh 2:7f.

From the vantage point of the memoirs of Ezra the two rebuildings were really one event, and it makes efforts to equate them. See the frustration of the rebuilding of the walls, Ezr 4:6-23, placed immediately after the frustration of the rebuilding of the temple, 4:1-5, even though that puts the former passage

---

1 Though the hand of the Chronicler can be seen in Ezra 1:2ff, the commentators accept that some such decree did exist. See Joseph Blenkinsopp, *Ezra-Nehemiah*, Old Testament Library (London: SCM, 1989) 74.

out of chronological sequence. Then the stoppage of work on the wall is actually placed right next to and even before the stoppage of work on the temple, 4:23f.

We have seen that when there is talk of the opposition from the surrounding peoples in connection with the building of God, Ps 48:5f; 83:7-9; 118:11-13, there is compelling evidence for placing those compositions at the project for the rebuilding of the walls. This serves to point up that it would be very difficult to have a formulation such as that found in vv 14-16a of the Song if it were written as early as the time of the temple rebuilding. Neither the Samaritans nor the surrounding peoples presented a vigorous threat to the rebuilding of the temple.

But the Song presents God the warrior defeating the surrounding peoples in the same way that he had carried out the primordial victory for his people in defeating the Egyptians. The Song represents a victory that is crucial to the Israelites; it has the same importance as the victory whereby they were saved from extinction and formed as a people. This victory of God over the surrounding peoples is a formulation that really only applies to a time when they constituted a critical threat, that victory whereby they were unable to stop the rebuilding of the walls.

The author of the Song of the Sea has used the peoples mentioned in the exodus to portray the enemies of the rebuilding. These are the enemies cited in Neh 4:1. The dwellers of the Canaan would mean those inhabitants of the cis-Jordan in the original land of the Canaanites. Thus, it would indicate the Samaritans, whose leader was Sanballat, cf 6:1. The Edomite residents of the South are the Arabians and their leader Geshem, cf 6:1. The dwellers of the central trans-Jordan under their leader Tobiah are the equivalent of the Moabites, cf Neh 2:10, 19. And the Ashdodites are the dwellers of Philistia. See also

Ezr 4:17-23. It is in this context that there is the real representation of a defeat for these peoples brought about by what God
has done, Neh 6:16.

Also, the sense of ease and security in the face of the surrounding peoples that the Song portrays, vv 13-17, and the
notion that by this victory God has established his never ending
rule, v 18, are very difficult to propose before the walls are
complete. The state of the walls still in ruin leaves the Israelites
a prey to the surrounding peoples, Ezr 4:4, 23; Neh 1:3, but in
the Song the defeat of the enemies is something already carried
out.

Also, access to the completed text of Ex 14, which seems
demanded by the evidence, cannot take place before the return
of Ezra, which would rule out the time of the temple building
but would dovetail very nicely into the time period of the Nehemiah's building project. That, of course, presupposes that the
date of 458 that the Scripture gives is indeed correct. That date
has been questioned since the time of A. Hoonacker, but recent
criticism discounts his arguments[2]. Thus the general conclusion
is that the Song reflects the period at or shortly after the rebuilding
of the walls in 444 B. C.

Authorship

This section posits that the whole of the Song of the Sea, the
psalm, the prose explanation, and the liturgical rubrics, come
from within the cult Levites. The psalm itself was a composition

---

2 D. A. Clines, *Ezra, Nehemiah, Esther*, New Century Bible Commentary
   (Grand Rapids: Eerdmans, 1984) 16-24. Clines refutes Hoonacker's
   arguments one by one. See also H. G. M. Williamson, *Ezra, Nehemiah*,
   Word Biblical Commentary 16 (Waco: Word Books, 1985) xxxix-xliv;
   Blenkinsopp 141-144.

of the Levitical singers. The real authors were the Asaphites. The composers of the liturgical rubrics and prose explanation were teaching Levites, distinct from the singers.

The role of the Levitical teachers in the composition

It can be affirmed that the Song of the Sea is not a redaction of an earlier, pre-exilic, work. A review of the evidence shows that there is nothing within the psalm that does not demonstrate substantial evidence of exclusively late usages. The psalm as a whole shows a consistent and well integrated unity of post-exilic thought patterns. One can speak of the roots of the psalm, but in terms of phrasing the roots stretch no further back than the Deuteronomistic redactors.

Now the caretakers of the D tradition after the Deuteronomistic period were the Levites. They considered themselves the teaching successors to Moses, Dt 31:9ff. They were to preserve the Torah, the teaching. By this is certainly meant the D law codes as preserved and recited in the Northern shrines, but it must certainly also refer to the historical teaching about the exodus and conquest as set forth in the D tradition.

This function of teacher of the tradition remains within the Levitical clans through the exile and into the post-exile. Thus they appear in the time of Ezra and Nehemiah performing the same functions with which they were charged in Dt 31:9ff, to read from the book of the Law and explain it on the feast of Succoth. They teach from the Law and explain it to the people, Neh 8:7-9, on the feast of Succoth, 8:14-18.

And the function of expert on the traditions was also carried out by the Levites during the exile, see Ezr 8:18f. It can, therefore, be assumed that the post-Deuteronomic redaction of the D corpus was also performed by these Levites.

Now in the Song of the Sea there is the demonstration of an intimate knowledge of Deuteronomistic and post-Deuteronomic texts. But our Song not only has knowledge of texts concerning the Jordan River crossing and the fear of the peoples, it is also the immersed in the tradition and theological viewpoint that went with them. Since the passages involved are fairly well dispersed in Dt and Js, they could not be picked out simply by a knowledge of the written scrolls. The Song of the Sea demonstrates an intimate contact with the last redactive layers and their viewpoints. Thus the composers of the Song had to have access to the living interpretation; that is, they could not simply know the text; they had to know the living tradition as well. Thus the composition has to be part of the milieu of the Levitical experts on the Deuteronomistic traditions.

Now the Sons of Asaph and the other singing clans cannot be the ultimate source of this tradition transmission and development. They do not belong to those groups who were Levites before the return, for none of the singing choirs were considered Levites immediately upon the return, Ezr 2:41 = Neh 7:44. Ezra 3:10 calls the Sons of Asaph, the leading choir, Levites by the time of the construction of the altar soon after the return. If that text is a true representation of the situation, then they reached Levitical status very quickly. But it is clear that even they were not considered Levites in the exile.

But the Levites who perform functions as teachers and cult leaders under the leadership of the family of Jeshua, Neh 9:4f, see also 8:7, do have their family names appear in the original lists of returned Levites, Ezr 2:40 = Neh 7:43. See also Ezr 8:18 which verifies that Sherebiah was known as a Levite in the exile, then see Neh 9:4; 8:7.

These men, though they were cult leaders, were not psalmists, and are not actual composers of the Song section, but it is to them that the intense knowledge of Deuteronomistic tradition demonstrated in the Song must ultimately be traced. The singers certainly also developed these traditions, but it is a tradition they absorbed from within the wider cultic milieu of the teaching Levites as they were themselves admitted into Levitical status.

The Levite teachers do meet all the requirements for the composers of the prose material around the Song. They are both leaders and arrangers of the cult, Neh 8:11; 9:4f; 12:8, 24, and teachers who are expert in explaining the scriptures, 8:7, and are especially at home in D. Thus they qualify as the writers of a framework that comprises a set of rubrics for cult performance and an explanation based in the tradition, both of which betray a very close familiarity with the D source material and the D point of view.

The teaching Levites are the caretakers of confessional literature about the sea crossing that was represented as being recited first by Moses, Dt 11:1-9, and a crossing and conquest tradition which sought to show that everything had its origin in Moses. The Song that is to be sung will be performed by other Levitical successors to Moses. From this entire point of view comes the rubric that attributes the Song of the Sea to Moses the Levite, who is the composer and performer of the Song.

The Levitical singer is styled the sister of Aaron. It is these Levites who considered themselves to be brothers of the priests.

They are specialists in explanation of Scripture in a semi-poetic manner, Neh 9:5-37. In that recitation they arrive at a formulation that closely resembles a line that appears in the explanation that accompanies the Song; compare Neh 9:11a with Ex 15:19b. This very well accounts for the explanation and its semi-poetic character. The character of the explanation is very close to P but formulates like the D traditions. The piece, therefore, has all of the marks of something written by Levites deeply rooted in the Deuteronomic tradition and who were in constant contact with the priests.

They arrange for the reading of Scripture to be part of overall cult ceremonies, Neh 9:3. The arrangers of the prose framework have placed the Song in its present position so that it can be used to convert the reading of the exodus story to the cult.

They have composed rubrics that are a virtual copy of the victory song in 1 Sm 18:6f. Its placement in this position is in accordance with the framework that considers the Song of the Sea to be a victory song, because it is common for a victory song to follow directly upon the prose account. Thus the authors of the framework demonstrate themselves to be experts and specialists in all the correct rubrics necessary for this cult piece, that is, Levitical cult leaders.

It can be concluded that the whole of the prose framework, both the rubrics and the prose summary, was written by these teaching Levites.

The Asaphite nature of the Song section

In the examination of the Song we have seen that every line traces back to the Levitical singing clans of the post-exile. We have also noted that there are several influences which taken together really define the entire poetic style and conceptual mentality of the piece. In vv 7-17 the presence of the Asaphites is overwhelming. Every verse has a definite correlation to Asaphite usages, and very frequently only Asaphite usages. The other influences are present in vv 1b-5, 18, 21b: these are the Levitical singers as a whole, the psalmic redactors found in first Isaiah, and the Levitical teachers.

The presence of the Levitical singers is clearly noted in vv 2, 4, 5, 6. The forms and usages of these lines occur elsewhere in psalms that have their הוֹדוּ chant, Ps 118; 136:15; 107:24, 26. Also, the only pure instances of the form of v 3 is found in the context of this chant, Jer 33:2, 11.

This chant, "Give thanks to the Lords for he is good, his love endures forever," occurs in Ps 106, 107, 118, 136. It is attributed at times to the singing groups as a whole. But it is primarily identified with the clan of Asaph. They are the ones who perform it in Ezr 3:10f. In later texts it is often referred to the singing choirs in general but always with the notion that the Asaphites are the chief performers. 1 Chr 16:41 mentions the Levitical singers Heman and Jeduthun who have the function of singing the refrain at the tent in Gibeah, but the leaders and principle performers are the Asaphites, who perform the chant before the ark in Jerusalem, 16:34, 7. In 2 Chr 5:12f the Asaphites are mentioned as the first of the three choirs who perform. The prophetic liturgy of 2 Chr 20 mentions the performance of the singing choirs in general, including those of the Kohathites and the Korahites, 20:21, 19, but the chief performer is an Asaphite, 20:14. These texts reflect the notion that the Sons of Asaph were the chief singing clan in the post-exilic period[3], Neh 11:17. So that when this refrain is present, it is very likely that we are in the presence of the Asaphites or within the sphere of their influence.

Vv 1b*a*, 2, 3, 18 are very closely tied to the authors of the redactional material present in first Isaiah. These redactive additions have already been shown to be very similar to the Levitical Ps 118, enough so that I have entertained the possibility of common literary circles. We can then note that where the material

---

3 Hartmut Gese, "Zür Geschichte der Kultsänger am zweiten Temple," in
   Vom Sinai zum Zion, Beitrage zür evangelischen Theolgie 64 (München:
   Chr. Kaiser, 1974) 147-158. He maintains that they eventually lost that
   position to the Korahites, but at a time long beyond the period of interest
   to us.

is not held in common with Ps 118, it very often has the character of Asaphite composition. Compare Is 12:2ab with Ps 78:53a. Then the initial phrase of the ensuing psalmic piece, Is 12:4-6, begins with the initial phrase ascribed to the Asaphite choirs at the beginning of their history, compare Is 12:4a*β*b*a* with 1 Chr 16:8; Ps 105:1. Is 12:4b*a* can also be compared with Ps 77:15b. Or Is 12:4a*β*b*a* can also be compared with its negative counterpart in Ps 79:6a*β*b. Then Is 25:1 contains the phrase עשׂה פלא. That appears otherwise only in the Song, in the Asaphite Ps 77:15; 78:12, and in the Hemanite Ps 88:11.

If Is 25:1 is taken within its redactive context, it describes the thanksgiving of Yahweh in which he is exalted and his wonders proclaimed. This is done among his elders in Jerusalem, 24:23. This can be compared with the scene of Ps 107:30-32. Yahweh is thanked, v 31, and exalted, v 32, for his wonders, v 31, in the gathering of the elders, v 32, in Jerusalem, v 30. The concept is the same and the vocabulary matches exactly. In the psalmic redactors of Isaiah you have the mind of the Levitical choirs, and are never too distant from the mind of the Asaphites.

The only phrasing in the Song that falls outside of the Asaphite sphere is one phrase in v 5, where the point of contact is with the Levitical teaching exposition of Neh 9:11b. It is very easy to see how there could be a sharing of tradition between the Levitical teachers and the Levitical singers. So that vv 1b-5, 18, 21b, also trace back to the Asaphites sphere.

It can then also be demonstrated that on the conceptual and functional level the formulaic enclosure is of the Asaphite mind. We first note that there are two places in the Old Testament where the Song of the Sea is mentioned, Ps 105:43; 106:12. Both of these psalms are Asaphite.

The authors of the opening lines of the Song of the Sea meant to place it after Ex 14, as part of the conversion of the reading of the exodus account to the cult. This mentality is present in Ps 106. Ps 106:12 makes sure to let the reader know that the Song of the Sea came directly after the Sea crossing. He presents it in its present position after the P redacted version of Ex 14. Compare Ps 106:11a, "the water covered them," with Ex 14:28a (P); Ps 106:11b, "not one of them was left," with 14:28b (P). Then 106:12 embraces both the last line of Ex 14 and the first line of the Song, compare וַיַּאֲמִינוּ in 106:12a and 14:31b, and יָשִׁירוּ in 106:12b with 15:1a.

So that the Asaphites who wrote Ps 106 present the original Israelites breaking out into cult song at the moment of the crossing. That is certainly the cult mentality of the authors of the opening lines of the Song of the Sea, because they consider it liturgically correct that the Israelite congregation of their day should break into song after the recitation of the passage of the Israelites in Ex 14.

We have also seen that the authors of the opening lines of the Song envisioned it to be a processional. The Asaphite author of Ps 105 considers that the Song of the Sea is a processional that reenacts the original procession of the exodus. He presents it as cult joy as the Israelites are "brought out" of Egypt by God, Ps 105:43.

Thus, every part of the Song is traceable to the Asaphites. They are responsible for its construction for placement after Ex 14. They are the authors of the opening lines that are formulas for insertion of the Song into its present position and that are used for processional entrance. Both parts of the Song are from their hand, and the juxtaposition of the themes of sea deliverance text and pastoral leading text are also specific to them. If it can be entertained that the other singing choirs contributed to the effort, it cannot be in any substantial way. The overall conception which embraces every verse of the Song is Asaphite.

The basic theology of the Asaphites is present in the Song. The Song of the Sea speaks about the base events of exodus and conquest, but in such a way that it portrays and explains the present situation. Not only does its portrayal of the past depict the present, it also forms the basis for the present. What God did then he is doing now. This is a general characteristic of Asaphite literature. They like to have recourse to base events or other events of the distant past to explain the present situation. One can see the operation of the Asaphite mind in Ps 77. The psalmist speaks of an unidentified difficult situation whose explanation is opaque to his mind, vv 4f. Then he seeks to solve it by recourse to ancient events, vv 6f, especially the exodus, 12f, 17-21, with an implicit assuredness that the power displayed there will be redone, vv 14-16.

Or the Asaphite authors of Ps 78 will describe the loss of the ark, v 60, the death of Phineas, 64a, his wife's death in childbirth where she cares only for the ark and not for her dead husband, 64b, the plague of hemorrhoids inflicted on the Philistines, 66a, etc. All leads up to the base event, the foundation of the cult in Jerusalem. But all is done in such a way so as to portray the destruction of the temple, the captivity, the restoration, and the legitimacy of the Jerusalem cult in the face of the Samaritans.

Similarly, Ps 83 represents the collusion of all the peoples of the satrapy Beyond the River, who had opposed the rebuilding of the walls. But it does so by using names of very ancient peoples to describe them, vv 7f, the Ishmaelites, Hagarites, etc. And it draws analogies to the time of the Judges, vv 10-12.

In Ps 74 the present state of the temple rests on what God did at the exodus. The action of God then is guarantee that it can be repeated now. Thus, the basis for the plea for rebuilding of the ruined temple, 74:1-10, is the creative action that he displayed at the exodus, vv 12-17. Ps 80 rests its plea for the ruined walls, v 13, on the fact that God had established them at the time of the exodus and conquest, vv 9-12.

The Song also demonstrates the same characteristic. It tells of the defeat of the Egyptians at the sea crossing and the entrance into Canaan, but in such a way that you can see the liberation from exile, return, and the rebuilding of the temple and city walls. The power he demonstrated then is the same power he has demonstrated now. In calling on this power the psalmist in 74:12 calls God "my king from of old." The kingship of Yahweh has been demonstrated in the power over the whole of the cosmos once in creation, but it is constantly repeated in his acts of salvation. The psalmist in the Song of the Sea celebrates that the power of the beginning events has been clearly repeated in the events that have allowed for the restoration of the city. In the enactment of this event the eternal power of God as king has been revealed. Hence v 18 celebrating the eternal kingship of Yahweh is an apt summary of the entire Song.

Final Remarks

Once it is established that the Song of the Sea was written at the same time as the prose framework, that they were both part of one coordinated effort, and that both were composed for insertion after Ex 14, then various things can be said with certainty. The Song of the Sea is a hymn, but specifically a victory song. This is established by the fact that the writers of the prose framework used a form that was obviously patterned on the singing of victory songs. The Song of the Sea is a Passover song because it was written for performance after the recitation of the exodus account.

It is not specifically a thanksgiving song, because it uses material found in thanksgiving works but adapts it to a hymn and praise form. It was not written for the autumn festival; although it could have also at some time been sung there.

The Song of the Sea knew the redacted version of Ex 14 and was written to recount the same event, as the P writer had formulated it. But it is not in the tradition stream of the J, E, or P sources there present. It has its base in D and flows from the D traditions, but it is not D, it is post D. It never has real influence from the pre-Deuteronomistic levels, but has a strong relation to the Deuteronomistic levels throughout.

Both parts one and two are influenced consistently by Dt-Isaiah. The authors are one of the post-exilic groups that carry on the traditions of that school. The influence of the other successor schools to the prophets are also present. Most important of these are the redactors found in the book of the consolations of Jeremiah. The liturgical mentality of third Isaiah and other post-exilic Isaian texts is also present.

The Song has a very close relationship to confessional literature, but only in its late form. It is also part of the movement that has applied myth to the exodus account. The myth usage is one which embraces both water chaos victory stories and temple building motifs. It has used the whole sweep of the myth story to show how the reenactment of the power God manifested in the beginning can explain the new exodus of the return and the new building of God's palace residence which is evidenced in the reconstruction of the temple and the city walls.

It has developed the story of the fear of the Canaanites and expanded it to include the surrounding peoples. Their paralysis in the face of the Israelite entrance into Canaan functions to demonstrate the inability of the surrounding peoples to prevent the reentrance of the Israelites into the land and the rebuilding of city and temple.

The whole of the formulations found in the Song can be fully explained by recourse to the Levites of the temple cult in the post-exile. The clan of the Sons of Asaph are the essential authors of the Song. Their influence is very strongly present in every part of the Song, and the overall structure and theology of the Song is specific to their school. This does not exclude the possibility that other clans took part in its composition, but the overall coordination of the writing of the Song portion can only be attributed to the Sons of Asaph.

The prose framework is from the cult Levitical teachers who were organizers of liturgical feast celebrations. The very close interaction between the singers and the teachers accounts for the strong presence of Deuteronomistic and post-Deuteronomic themes in the Song. The overall conception of a Song composed for its present function of liturgical celebration of the exodus is to be attributed to the cooperation of the Levitical singers and teachers.

WORKS CITED

Anderson, A. A. *2 Samuel*. Word Biblical Commentary 11. Waco: Word Books, 1989.

Baentsch, Bruno. *Exodus, Leviticus, und Numeri.* Handkommentar zum Alten Testamentum. Göttingen: Vandenhoeck and Ruprecht, 1903.

Baudissin, Wolf Wilhelm. *Einleitung in die Bucher des Alten Testamentes.* Leipzig: S. Hirzel, 1901.

Bauer, Hans and Pontus Leander. *Historische Grammatik der Hebräischen Sprache des Alten Testamentes.* Hildesheim: Georg Olms, 1962.

Bender, Adolf. "Das Lied Exodus 15." *Zeitschrift für die alttestamentliche Wissenschaft* 23 (1903): 1-48.

Bernini, Giuseppi. *Sofonia -Gioele - Abdia - Giona.* Nuovissima Versione della Bibbia. Roma: Paoline, 1972.

Beyerlin, Walter. *Werden und Wesen des 107 Psalms.* Beihefte zur Zeitschrift für die alttestamentliche Wissenschaft 153. Berlin: de Gruyter, 1978.

Blenkinsopp, Joseph. *Ezra-Nehemiah.* The Old Testament Library. London: SCM, 1989.

Botterweck, G. Johannes and Helmer Ringgren, eds. *Theological Dictionary of the Old Testament*, vol 4. Trans. David Green. Grand Rapids: Eerdmans, 1980.

Briggs, C. A. *The Book of Psalms.* 2 vols. The International Critical Commentary. Edinburgh: T and T Clark, 1906-7.

Brown, Francis, S. R. Driver, and Charles A. Briggs, eds. *A Hebrew and English Lexicon of the Old Testament.* Oxford: Oxford UP, 1951.

Budd, Philip J. *Numbers.* Word Biblical Commentary 5. Waco: Word Books, 1984.

Burney, C. F. *The Book of Judges.* The Library of Biblical Studies. New York: KTAV, 1970.

Butler, Trent Craver. "'The Song of the Sea': Exodus 15:1-8: A Study in the Exegesis of Hebrew Poetry." Diss. Vanderbilt U, 1971.

---. *Joshua.* Word Biblical Commentary 17. Waco: Word Books, 1983.

Carroll, Robert P. *Jeremiah: A Commentary.* Old Testament Library. Philadelphia: Westminster, 1986.

Clements, R. E. *Isaiah 1-39.* New Century Bible Commentary. Grand Rapids: Eerdmans, 1980.

Clines, D. A. *Ezra, Nehemiah, Esther.* New Century Bible Commentary. Grand Rapids: Eerdmans, 1984.

Coats, George W. "History and Theology in the Sea Tradition." *Studia Theologica* 29 (1975): 53-62.

---. "The Song of the Sea." *Catholic Biblical Quarterly* 31 (1969): 1-17.

Cornill, Carl. *Introduction to the Canonical Books of the Old Testament.* Trans. G. H. Box. New York: Putnam's, 1907.

Crimm, Keith, ed. *The Interpreter's Dictionary of the Bible.* Abingdon: Nashville, 1976.

Cross, Frank Moore. "The Divine Warrior in Israel's Early Cult." *Biblical Motifs*. Ed. Alexander Altmann. Lown Institute Studies and Texts 7. Cambridge, Mass.: Harvard UP, 1966. 11-30.

---. "The Song of the Sea and Canaanite Myth." *God and Christ: Existence and Providence*. Ed. Robert W. Funk, et al. Journal for Theology and Church 5. New York: Harper, 1968. 1-25. Rpt. in *Canaanite Myth and Hebrew Epic: Essays in the History of the Religion of Israel*. Harvard: Harvard UP, 1973. 112-144.

Cross, Frank M., and David Noel Freedman. "The Song of Miriam." *Journal of Near Eastern Studies* 14 (1955): 237-250.

Childs, Brevard S. *The Book of Exodus*. Old Testament Library. Philadelphia: Westminster, 1974.

---. "A tradition-Historical Study of the Reed Sea Tradition." *Vetus Testamentum* 20 (1970): 406-418.

Elliger, K., and W. Rudolph, eds. *Biblia Hebraica Stuttgartensia*. Stuttgart: Deutsche Bibelstiftung, 1966-77.

Fohrer, Georg. *Uberlieferung und Geschichte des Exodus*. Berlin: Alfred Topelmann, 1964.

Foresti, Fabrizio. "Composizione e Redazione Deuteronomistica in Ex 15,1-18." *Lateranum* 48 (1982): 41-69.

Freedman, David Noel. "Early Israelite History in the Light of Early Israelite Poetry." *Unity and Diversity*. Ed. Hans Goedicke and J. M. Roberts. Baltimore: Johns Hopkins UP, 1975. 3-35. Rpt. in *Pottery, Poetry, and Prophecy: Studies in Early Hebrew Poetry*. Winona Lake, Indiana: Eisenbrauns, 1980. 131-66.

---. "Divine Names and Titles in Early Hebrew Poetry." *Magnalia Dei: The Mighty Acts of God*. Ed F. M. Cross, et al. New York: Doubleday, 1976. 55-107. Rpt. in *Pottery, Poetry, and Prophecy: Studies in Early Hebrew Poetry*. Winona Lake, Indiana: Eisenbrauns, 1980. 77-130.

---. "The Song of the Sea." *Pottery, Poetry, and Prophecy: Studies in Early Hebrew Poetry*. Winona Lake, Indiana: Eisenbrauns, 1980. 179-86.

---. "Strophe and Meter in Exodus 15." *A Light Unto My Path*. Ed. Howard N. Bream, Ralph D. Heim, and Carey A. Moore. Philadelphia: Temple UP, 1974. 163-203. Rpt. in *Pottery, Poetry, and Prophecy: Studies in Early Hebrew Poetry*. Winona Lake, Indiana: Eisenbrauns, 1980. 187-228.

Garofalo, Salvatore. "L'Epinicio di Mose." *Biblica* 18 (1937): 1-22.

Gese, Hartmut. "Zur Geschichte der Kultsänger am zweiten Temple." *Abraham unser Vater*. Fs. Otto Michel. Ed. M. Hengel and P. Schmidt. Leiden: E. J. Brill, 1963. 222-34. Rpt. in *Vom Sinai zum Zion*. Beiträge zur evangelischen Theolgie 64. München: Chr. Kaiser, 1974. 147-58.

Gibson, J. C. L. *Canaanite Myths and Legends*. 2nd ed. Edinburgh: T and T Clark, 1977.

Gray, George Buchanan. *The Book of Isaiah: I-XXVII*. The International Critical Commentary. Edinburgh: T and T Clark, 1912.

Gray, John. *1 And 2 Kings*. Old Testament Library. Philadelphia: Westminster, 1970.

---, *Joshua, Judges, Ruth*. New Century Bible Commentary. Grand Rapids: Eerdmans, 1986.

Haupt, Paul. "Moses' Song of Triumph." *American Journal of Semitic Languages* 20 (1904): 149-72.

Holm-Nielson, Svend. "The Exodus Tradition in Ps 105." *Annual of the Swedish Theological Institute* 11. Fs. G. Gerleman (1977-78): 22-30.

Holzinger, Heinrich. *Exodus*. Kurzer Hand-Commentar zum Alten Testament. Tubingen: J. C. B. Mohr, 1900.

Huesman, John E. "Exodus." *The Jerome Biblical Commentary*. Englewood Cliffs: Prentice Hall, 1968. 47-66.

Hyatt, James Philip. "The Book of Jeremiah." *The Interpreter's Bible*. Vol. 5. Nashville: Abingdon, 1956. 775-1142.

---. *A Commentary on Exodus*. New Century Bible London: Oliphants, 1971.

Jones, Gwilym H. *1 and 2 Kings*, vol 2. New Century Bible Commentary. Grand Rapids: Eerdmans, 1984.

Kaiser, Otto. *Isaiah 1-12: A Commentary*. Trans. R. A. Wilson. The Old Testament Library. Philadelphia: Westminster, 1972.

---. *Isaiah 13-39: A Commentary*. Trans. R. A. Wilson. The Old Testament Library. Philadelphia: Westminster, 1974.

---. *Einleitung in des Alte Testament 5*. Gütersloh: Gerd Mohn, 1984.

Kautzsch, E. *Gesenius' Hebrew Grammar*. Trans. A. E. Cowley. 2nd ed. Oxford: Clarendon, 1910.

Kirkpatrick, A. F. *The Book of Psalms*. Cambridge: Cambridge UP, 1902. Grand Rapids: Baker, 1982.

Kohata, Fujiko. *Jahwist und Priesterschrift in Exodus 3-14*. Beihefte zur Zeitschrift für die alttestamentliche Wissenschaft 166. Berlin: de Gruyter, 1986.

Lindblom, J. *Prophecy in Ancient Israel*. Philadelphia: Fortress, 1962.

Lohfink, N. "Deuteronomy" *The Interpreter's Dictionary of the Bible*. Supplementary Vol. Nashville: Abingdon, 1976. 229-32.

May, Herbert G. "The Book of Ezekiel." *The Interpreter's Bible* Vol. 6. Nashville: Abingdon, 1956. 39-338.

Mayes, A. D. H. *Deuteronomy*. New Century Bible. Grand Rapids: Eerdmans, 1981.

---. *The Story of Israel between Settlement and Exile*. London: SCM Press, 1983.

Mays, James L. *Micah*. The Old Testament Library. Philadelphia: Westminster, 1976.

McCarter, P. Kyle. *II Samuel*. The Anchor Bible. Garden City: Doubleday, 1984.

McCullough, W. Steward. "The Book of Psalms." *The Interpreter's Bible*. Vol. 6. Nashville: Abingdon, 1955. 1-763.

Miller, J. Maxwell, and Gene M. Tucker. *The Book of Joshua*. The Cambridge Bible Commentary. Cambridge: Cambridge UP, 1974.

Moore, George F. *Judges*. The International Critical Commentary. Edinburgh: T and T Clark, 1895

Moran, S. L. "Deuteronomy." *A New Catholic Commentary on Holy Scripture*. Rev. ed. Surrey: Nelson, 1975. 256-276.

Moriarty, Frederick L. "Numbers." *The Jerome Biblical Commentary*. Englewood Cliffs: Prentice Hall, 1968. 86-100.

Mowinckel, Sigmund. *Der Achtundsechzigste Psalm*. Oslo: 1953.

---. *Psalmenstudien I-II*. 1921-24. Amsterdam: P. Schippers, 1961.

Muilenburg, James. "A Liturgy on the Triumphs of Yahweh." *Studia Biblica et Semitica*. Fs T. C. Vriezen. Wageningen: H. Veenman, 1966. 233-51.

Murphy, Roland E. "Psalms." *The Jerome Biblical Commentary.* Englewood Cliffs: Prentice Hall, 1968. 569-602.

Myers, Jacob M. "The Book of Judges." *The Interpreter's Bible.* Vol. 2. Nashville: Abingdon, 1953. 675-826.

The New Jerusalem Bible. Garden City: Doubleday, 1985.

Nicholsen, Ernest W. *Deuteronomy and Tradition.* Oxford: Basil Blackwell, 1967.

Noth, Martin. *Exodus.* Trans. J. S. Bowden. The Old Testament Library. Philadelphia: Westminster, 1962.

---. *Numbers: A Commentary.* Trans. James D. Martin. The Old Testament Library. Philadelphia: Westminster, 1968.

Oesterley, W. O. E. *Ancient Hebrew Poems.* London: SPCK, 1938.

Pfeiffer, Robert H. *Introduction to the Old Testament.* New York: Harper, 1941.

Phillips, Anthony. *Deuteronomy.* The Cambridge Bible Commentary. Cambridge: Cambridge UP, 1973.

Pritchard, James B., ed. *Ancient Near Eastern Texts.* 3rd ed. Princeton: Princeton UP, 1969.

Ravasi, Gianfranco. *Il Libro dei Salmi: Commento e Attualizzazione.* 3 vols. Bologna: Dehoniane, 1981-84.

Rozelaar, Marc. "The Song of the Sea." *Vetus Testamentum* 2 (1952): 221-228.

Rylaarsdam, J. Coert. "The Book of Exodus." *The Interpreter's Bible.* Vol. 1. Nashville: Abingdon, 1952. 831-1099.

Schmidt, Hans. "Das Meerlied. Ex 15:2-19." *Zeitschrift für die alttestamentliche Wissenschaft* 49 (1931), 59-66.

Schreiner, Josef. *Sion-Jerusalem. Jahwe's Königssits.* Studien sum Alten und Neuen Testament. Vol. 7. Munich: Kosel-Verlag, 1963.

Smith, George Adam. *The Early Poetry of Israel in its Physical and Social Origins.* London: Oxford UP, 1912.

Smith, John. *Micah, Zephaniah and Nahum.* The International Critical Commentary. Edinburgh: T and T Clark, 1912.

Snaith, N. H. *Leviticus and Numbers.* The Century Bible. London: Nelson, 1967.

Staerk, Willi. *Die Schriften des Alten Testaments.* Vol. 3: Lyrik. Gottingen: Vandenhoeck, 1911.

Strauss, Hans. "Das Meerlied des Mose--ein 'Siegeslied' Israels?" *Zeitschrift fur die alttestamentliche Wissenschaft* 97 (1985): 103-9.

Tournay, R. "Recherches sur la Chronologie des Psaumes." Revue Biblique 65 (1958): 321-57.

Vaux, Roland de. *Ancient Israel its Life and Institutions.* Trans. John McHugh. London: Darton, Longman and Todd, 1961.

---. *The Early History of Israel.* Trans. David Smith. 2 vols. London: Darton, Longman and Todd, 1978.

Vries, Simon J. De. *1 Kings.* Word Biblical Commentary 12. Waco: Word Books, 1985.

Watts, John D. "The Song of the Sea--Ex. XV." *Vetus Testamentum* 7 (1957): 371-380.

---. *The Books of Joel, Obadiah, Jonah, Nahum, Habakkuk and Zephaniah.* Cambridge: Cambridge UP, 1975.

---. *Isaiah 1-33.* Word Biblical Commentary 24. Waco: Word Books, 1983.

---. *Isaiah 34-66*, Word Biblical Commentary 25, Waco: Word Books, 1987.

Weinfeld, Moshe. *Deuteronomy and the Deuteronomic School.* Oxford: Clarendon, 1972.

Weippert, H. "Pferd und Streitwagen." *Biblisches Reallexikon.* Ed. Kurt Galling. Tubingen: J. C. B. Mohr, 1977. 250-54.

Williamson, H. G. M. *Ezra, Nehemiah.* Word Biblical Commentary 16 Waco: Word Books, 1985.

Wolfe, Rolland E. "The Book of Micah." *The Interpreter's Bible.* Vol. 6. Nashville: Abingdon, 1956. 895-949.

Zimmerli, Walther. *Ezekiel 2.* Trans. James D. Martin. Hermeneia. Philadelphia: Fortress, 1979-83.

BEIHEFTE ZUR ZEITSCHRIFT FÜR DIE ALTTESTAMENTLICHE WISSENSCHAFT

Prophet und Prophetenbuch
Festschrift für Otto Kaiser zum 65. Geburtstag
Herausgegeben von
Volkmar Fritz · Karl-Friedrich Pohlmann · Hans-Christoph Schmitt
Groß-Oktav. VII, 284 Seiten. Mit einem Frontispiz. 1989.
Ganzleinen DM 144,–   ISBN 3 11 011339 2 (Band 185)

KÅRE BERGE
Die Zeit des Jahwisten
Ein Beitrag zur Datierung jahwistischer Vätertexte
Groß-Oktav. XI, 329 Seiten. 1990. Ganzleinen DM 148,–
ISBN 3 11 011892 0 (Band 186)

CHRISTOF HARDMEIER
Prophetie im Streit vor dem Untergang Judas
Erzählkommunikative Studien zur Entstehungssituation der
Jesaja- und Jeremiaerzählungen in II Reg 18–20 und Jer 37–40
Groß-Oktav. XVII, 506 Seiten. 1990. Ganzleinen DM 178,–
ISBN 3 11 011735 5 (Band 187)

LUDGER SCHWIENHORST-SCHÖNBERGER
Das Bundesbuch (Ex 20,22–23,33)
Studien zu seiner Entstehung und Theologie
Groß-Oktav. XIV, 468 Seiten. 1990. Ganzleinen DM 168,–
ISBN 3 11 012404 1 (Band 188)

ERHARD BLUM
Studien zur Komposition des Pentateuch
Groß-Oktav. X, 433 Seiten. 1990. Ganzleinen DM 148,–
ISBN 3 11 012027 5 (Band 189)

Preisänderungen vorbehalten

Walter de Gruyter Berlin · New York

BEIHEFTE ZUR ZEITSCHRIFT FÜR DIE ALTTESTAMENTLICHE WISSENSCHAFT

HERBERT NIEHR
Der höchste Gott
Alttestamentlicher JHWH-Glaube im Kontext syrisch-kanaanäischer Religion des 1. Jahrtausends v. Chr.

Groß-Oktav. X, 268 Seiten. 1990. Ganzleinen DM 98,–
ISBN 3 11 012342 8 (Band 190)

DWIGHT R. DANIELS
Hosea and Salvation History
The Early Traditions of Israel in the Prophecy of Hosea

1990. Large-octavo. IX, 148 pages. Cloth DM 78,–
ISBN 3 11 012143 3 (Volume 191)

UWE BECKER
Richterzeit und Königtum
Redaktionsgeschichtliche Studien zum Richterbuch

Groß-Oktav. IX, 326 Seiten. 1990. Ganzleinen DM 118,–
ISBN 3 11 012440 8 (Band 192)

DONG HYUN BAK
Klagender Gott – klagende Menschen
Studien zur Klage im Jeremiabuch

Groß-Oktav. XIII, 273 Seiten. 1990. Ganzleinen DM 104,–
ISBN 3 11 012341 X (Band 193)

INGO KOTTSIEPER
Die Sprache der Aḥiqarsprüche
Groß-Oktav. XII, 302 Seiten. Mit 9 Falttafeln. 1990.
Ganzleinen DM 124,–   ISBN 3 11 012331 2 (Band 194)

Preisänderungen vorbehalten

Walter de Gruyter   **Berlin · New York**

GTU Library
2400 Ridge Road
Berkeley, CA 94709
For renewals call (510) 649-2500

All items are subject to recall.